BEYOND THE WHITE NOISE

BEYOND THE WHITE NOISE

Mission in a Multicultural World

Tom Montgomery-Fate

Chalice Press
ST. LOUIS, MISSOURI

All of the author's royalties from the sale of this book are being donated to *Pintig*, a Filipino drama and arts group in Chicago, and to the Asia Pacific Center for Justice and Peace in Washington, D.C.

Cover artwork: Marcel Zellweger

Cover design: Michael Domínguez

10 9 8 7 6 5 4 3 2 1   97 98 99 00 01 02

Library of Congress Cataloging–in–Publication Data

Montgomery-Fate, Tom.
      Beyond the white noise : mission in a multicultural world   / Tom
Montgomery-Fate.
      p.   cm.
      ISBN 0-8272-0223-7
      1. Montgomery-Fate, Tom.   2. Missionaries—Philippines—
Biography.   3. Missionaries—United States—Biography.   4. Christianity and culture—Philippines.   5. Multiculturalism—Religious aspects—
Christianity.   6. Missions.   I. Title.
      BV3382.M66A3   1997   97-6390
      266—dc21   CIP

*For
Luna
Dingayan*

Acknowledgments

M any people helped to make this book possible. Thanks to Lita Calilan, a gentle teacher, for her daily invitations into Ilokano culture; to Cobbie Palm, for his cross-cultural insight and guidance; to Luna and Perla Dingayan, Digna and Juancho Campañano, Daniel Gaces, and Gloria Santos, colleagues and friends, for their ongoing support in Laoag; and to my students at Northern Christian College, for all they taught and still teach me about listening and culture crossing.

Thanks to Carol Montgomery-Fate, who lived these stories with me, for her patience, her hard questions, and her attention to editorial detail; to Robert Schreiter, for helping me imagine how to turn a stack of journals into a book; to Cyndie DeRidder, Renny Golden, Harvey Lord, Susan Thistlethwaite, and Steven VanderStaay, for their encouragement and generous editorial assistance; to Doug Cunningham, Dan Dale, and Nancy Jones, former missionaries, for their experiential insights and related suggestions; to Laura Jakubowski, at College of DuPage, for her administrative updating and loyal correspondence during my time away.

Thanks to the Ragdale Foundation, for a quiet place to work; to College of DuPage, for supporting my extended leave; to the Asia Pacific Center for Justice and Peace in Washington, D.C., for their assistance in locating numerous articles and elusive bits of information; and to the journals where the following essays first appeared (sometimes under a modified title): *Manoa,* University of Hawaii Press ("The Rain Makes the Roof Sing"); *English International,* National Council of Teachers of English ("White Christmas," "Where Power Comes From"); *The Other Side* ("Beyond the White Noise," "Beyond White Privilege," "Philippine Christology," "Listening in South Dakota"); *Creation Spirituality* ("Waiting for the Kindom"); and *The Disciple* ("We've a Story to Hear from the Nations"). Leny Mendoza Strobel's essay "Undoing the Colonial Gaze" also appeared in *Amerasia Journal* (in an expanded format).

Special thanks to Delores Fate, Russell Fate, Jean Hermans, Chuck Jorgensen, Claude Marie Barbour, and Cleo Martin, mentors.

The Bible passages cited come from the *Christian Community Bible*, 4th ed., Claretian Publications, Quezon City, Philippines (1990).

Table of Contents

Foreword

O nce while traveling in the Philippines, I was invited to the home of some middle-class people from one of the churches my group and I were visiting. I was coming for lunch, and I was looking forward to a traditional Philippine meal. I was served Wonder Bread, canned ham, and, with great ceremony, a can of Dole pineapple in heavy syrup—which was brought to the table and opened, the soggy, super-sweet rounds of fruit ladled into an elaborate bowl.

As I smiled and chewed the foamy Wonder Bread, the rubbery canned ham, and the plastic pineapple round from the Dole can, I thought of the *pan de sal* I had eaten in the market, of the *lechon* (roast pig) in a poor community on Negros Orientale, and the thousands of pineapples I had seen growing fresh and huge in nearby fields—not far from where we were lunching on this travesty of American food. But my hosts were delighted to offer me these delicacies, all imported from the United States. They were obviously very proud of this meal. This is the colonialized heritage of the Philippines—this fascination with all things American. Most Filipinos cannot afford these imported goods—but they can see them in the mega malls Tom Montgomery-Fate eloquently describes. Wonder Bread on a pedestal, forever out of reach. But not out of mind. The desire is all the more debilitating for being unattainable.

It is difficult to understand the long and complicated history of colonization and what it does to the colonized and to the colonizer. This relationship is described in a work of fiction:

"It's what I never understand about the U. S., I guess."
"What?"
"The selfishness, like babies have. You don't ever realize that the rest of the world is obsessed with you. The Manila papers, since I have learned to read, are full of editorials—every day—on what

xi

America thinks, what America does, what is our relationship to America. It is like a love affair, you know, or something—we hate you when we feel rejected, we love you when you look at us, like you take us seriously." [1]

The gulf between my hosts and me was enormous. Politeness and respect dictated that I consume what was offered at face value—an expensive meal chosen with care for a valued guest. I could not tell them that I was choking on every bite, choking on my own country's colonial heritage that made them undervalue their own culture and its traditions and overvalue American culture. What could I say that would not embarrass and confuse my hosts? Should I ask for fresh, native pineapple and insult their offering?

Into this tortured history walks the missionary. Is he or she a "liberal"? Well then, the history can be discounted in favor of an immediate encounter between people. My hosts and I have our humanity in common. It should be enough. Is she or he a "conservative"? Then we are all in Christ, and communal history and even individual history are transcended in favor of eternity. Is he or she a liberation theologian? Well, then, we side with the poor and marginalized and work with them to transform the world.

But unfortunately, we are humans in history, and so who we are is constructed from that colonial heritage, despite our common humanity. We live in history now, not in some heaven that is paved with golden streets. And if we choose to take history seriously, as liberation theologians have, what happens *until* we transform the world? Tom Montgomery-Fate skips over none of these contradictions and complications.

---

[1] Barbara Wilson, *Murder in the Collective* (Seattle: Seal Press, 1984), p. 94, quoted in Rita Nakashima Brock and Susan Brooks Thistlethwaite, *Casting Stones: Prostitution and Liberation in Asia and the United States* (Minneapolis: Fortress Press, 1996), p. 53.

Mission has traditionally been conceived as doing for—an act of charity combined with evangelical outreach. Teaching, healing, preaching—these are its practices, and many of the practitioners did this work under difficult conditions out of love.

But love separated from justice can perpetrate serious harm. It is, even in its best examples, paternalism. The one loved does not get any say in the matter. The one loved doesn't even get a chance to be unlovable if that is his or her choice. He becomes an object, a possession.

The question this book addresses is whether we can ever cross cultural boundaries with integrity. Tom Montgomery-Fate leads us on a journey of listening with intensity to the sounds a culture makes when it is not being drowned out with good intentions. This is what he calls "co-mission."

Co-mission is a hard discipline. The hardest lesson is that not everything can be solved. I could not solve my own country's colonial heritage, nor my hosts' interpretation of American culture. I couldn't even address it. I had to be quiet and respect their hospitality. It is a difficult and sometimes fruitless exercise to try to sort these problems out.

So what are we to do? Well, first, don't *do* anything. Patiently, quietly, go with Tom Montgomery-Fate into co-mission in the Philippines, in Nicaragua, in Appalachia, in South Dakota, and learn to look, to be still, to listen beyond the white noise. And respect what is and is not possible.

Susan Brooks Thistlethwaite
Chicago Theological Seminary

FROM MISSION TO CO-MISSION

I

The Filipino people have had the misfortune of being "liberated" four times during their entire history. First came the Spaniards who "liberated" them from the "enslavement of the devil," next came the Americans who liberated them from Spanish oppression, then the Japanese who "liberated" them from American imperialism, then the Americans again who liberated them from the Japanese Fascists. After every "liberation" they found their country inhabited by foreign "benefactors."

Renato Constantino[1]

He may smite the hand that blesses him, but he must be blessed. We want to do it [even] if he doesn't want it done.

Bruce Kirshner,[2] a Disciples of Christ missionary to the Philippines (1905-1917)

A Story to Hear from the Nations

In 1968, I was in the third grade at Leslie Bell Elementary School in Lexington, Missouri. At recess, my best friend, Alan Dodson, pointed out a fact which I hoped he hadn't noticed: Jerome January was wearing my old "Coke: It's the Real Thing" T-shirt, and a pair of my old blue jeans. "Why's he wearing your clothes?" Alan asked, laughing. "Why don't he get his own?" I didn't have an answer. I felt embarrassed. Alan didn't like Jerome or any of the "coloreds," as he called them.

---

[1] Renato Constantino, *The Philippines: A Past Revisited*, vol.1, (Quezon City, Philippines: Renato Constantino, 1975) p. 11, cited in Eleazar Fernandez' *Toward a Theology of Struggle* (New York: Orbis, 1994), p. 8.

[2] Quoted in Kenton Clymer's, *Protestant Missionaries in the Philippines, 1898-1916* (Chicago: University of Illinois Press, 1986), p. 15.

Martin Luther King, Jr., had just been assassinated, and riots had broken out in nearby Kansas City, so there was some tension in Lexington—between the majority white community (including the "minutemen," a white supremacist organization) and the blacks who lived in a small, dilapidated section of town. That was where Jerome lived, with his mom and grandma and several brothers and sisters. Their small wooden house had a dirt floor. My mom, an elementary music teacher, had met Jerome's mom, a cook, in the school's hot lunch line. They had gotten to know each other. Every year we took them boxes of our old clothes. And in the summer the January kids sometimes went out with us for ice cream in our old grey Chevy. We had fun.

One night I told my Mom about Alan's teasing. She was unfazed. "Jerome's got as much right to a shirt and a pair of pants as anyone else," she said matter-of-factly. "He's wearing your old clothes because they're short on money right now." I was curious as to why *all* of the black families in Lexington seemed to be short on money, but I didn't ask. Mom went back to her lesson plans and I went to bed.

A year later I visited my brother on the west side of Kansas City. The morning after I arrived he invited me to join a picket line at a used car dealership in his neighborhood. The owners were quickly painting and souping up dumps and selling them at exorbitant prices to the poor people who lived in the community. As the long, slow string of black and white marchers slowly circled the dealership, the white owners became enraged and shouted threats. We picketed all morning. Several pickets and several weeks later, the dealership closed. As a nine-year-old walking in that picket line I felt some defiance and pride, but mostly I felt a profound sense of belonging, of hope.

In college I became involved in Central-American solidarity work and frequently visited the region. Uriel Molina, a Nicaraguan priest who had worked with the F.S.L.N. for many years in the war against U.S.-backed dictator Anastazio

Somoza, greatly inspired me.[3] Since I often stayed with a family who lived just down the street from Padre Uriel's church, I met with him many times. One day we talked about why he, at great personal risk, had decided to confront many of the Catholic hierarchy's conservative theological and political positions—to advocate liberation theology instead, and to support an armed revolution. Later in the discussion, trying to describe what he called the "Christian process," he quoted a Spanish poet: "Walker there is no road. We make the road by walking." And then, smiling, he put his arm around me. "Here in Nicaragua," he said, "we know that Christianity is not about *arriving*."

A decade later, shortly after my wife, Carol, and I had returned to the U.S. from a teaching assignment at a small college in the Philippines, these and other early cross-cultural experiences flooded my brain. We were attending an ecumenical conference on global mission. Along with other recently returned international missionaries, we gave reports to various denominational executives and mission board members. For the final hymn in the closing worship we sang, "We've a Story to Tell the Nations." The first stanza is revealing: "We've a story to tell the nations that shall turn their hearts to the right. A story of truth and mercy, a story of peace and light...."

While listening to others sing the song I was filled with the same questions with which I had struggled during the entire conference, and during much of our eighteen months in the Philippines. To whom does "the story" belong? Who can determine its "rightness" and "truth"? What does One-Third (or "First") World[4] missionaries "telling the story" have to do with the historic silencing of Two-Thirds (or "Third")

---

[3] The F.S.L.N. (The Sandinista Front for National Liberation) toppled the Somoza regime on July 19, 1979. I met with Padre Uriel in the mid 1980s, during the Sandinistas' ongoing war with the U.S.-backed Contras.

[4] I replace the traditional "First" and "Third" Worlds with "One-Third" and "Two-Thirds" Worlds in order to more accurately describe the global ratio of materially poor to materially rich people, and to suggest that rich countries shouldn't come "First" or be perceived as more "worthy."

World's voices, and with the loss of so many indigenous stories of faith? Who will turn whose heart?

Despite many spirit-filled moments, the conference left me wondering about mission jargon versus mission practice. Though many One-Third World churches in the U.S. have recently adopted less paternal, more cross-culturally sensitive mission language, in practice, many still fail to include or only minimally include Two-Thirds World representatives in the evolving dialogue about mission, culture, and historical justice. The One-Third World church in the U.S. struggles to listen to the Two-Thirds World, to our shared history and our growing interdependence. This *institutional* struggle to listen, to reconsider mission and mission history, was mirrored in our *individual* struggle to listen and come to terms with colonial mission in the Philippines.

Lila Watson, an aboriginal woman from Australia, is often quoted for the advice she once gave to white mission workers: "If you have come to help us you're wasting your time. But if you have come because your liberation is bound up with ours, then let us work together." She defines authentic partnership. She suggests that the one-way cross-cultural mission model suggested in the song lyrics above is destructive, that mission has little to do with a material "have" helping a material "have not," that mission is necessarily *co-mission:* a mutual process of risk and liberation, of co-building bridges of understanding over the vast ravines of racism and imperialism.

We eventually came to realize that the best way to enter and gain acceptance in our new community in the Philippines was not to tell our story, or *the* story, but instead to listen to the stories of our hosts. This was in part because they already knew our stories: the American story, the Christian story, and the mission story.[5] These stories were imposed

---

[5] This is not to suggest that the "American story" is the story of the W.A.S.P., or that all mission is/was destructive. Filipinos were required to know certain versions of these stories in order to survive. But there was/ is no reciprocity. Even today few Americans could name a city in the

on them via a conquest and colonization process which lasted over four hundred years. For four centuries their hearts and heads were turned and twisted, as their faith, culture, and national identity were forcibly defined and redefined for them. Their "stories of truth and mercy" were and are stories of courageous resistance, of communal suffering and surviving, of miraculous adaptation, of ingenious subversion and invention. They are stories that have both reimagined and preserved Filipino cultures.

In muddy rice fields, in markets overflowing with fish and conversation, in sweaty, packed *jeepneys*[6] and tricycles, in bobbing outrigger *bancas* on the South China Sea, in bamboo *nipa* huts, in isolated tribal villages, and in our classrooms, we listened to some of these stories. They still speak to us, long after our return to the U.S. They continue to turn our hearts and heads to a God who is known in an immense, intricate tapestry of cultures, communities, and faith traditions, a God who dwelled in the Philippines long before Magellan, MacArthur, and McDonald's.

These essays, adapted from memory and notes in my journals, attempt to document this turning.

Philippines (besides Manila), or the country's president, or describe the historic involvement of the U.S.

[6]For brief definitions of Filipino terms used in this book, see the Glossary beginning on p. 151.

Turning Hearts, Listening Hearts

Malakas ang bulong sa sigaw.
(A whisper may sometimes
seem louder than a shout.)

Tagalog proverb[1]

The Word of God cannot be heard in the
noisy world of today. And even if it
blazoned forth with all the panoply of
noise so that it could be heard in the
midst of all the other noise, then it would
no longer be the Word of God.
Therefore create silence.

Søren Kierkegaard [2]

Laoag, the town where we lived, is a provincial capital and rice farming community in the Ilocos region of Northern Luzon. The day after we arrived, I went for a walk to try to familiarize myself with the city. Most of the teenagers or adults I passed turned to stare at me. Eventually some would smile and call out "Hi Joe!" or "Americano!" Some of the smaller children would point and say *"puraw"* ("white") to their friends, to be sure they didn't miss me. One boy on a bicycle, who was craning back to get a better look at the newly arrived oddity he had just passed, rode into a *balete* tree. Two other little kids walked straight into a bougainvillea bush.

[1] Quoted in Rebecca Asedillo and B. David Williams, *The Sari Sari Store* (New York: Friendship Press, 1989), p. 72.
[2] Quoted in Nick Bonzanic's essay, "Patience," *Manoa* (Honolulu: University of Hawaii Press, Summer, 1995, vol. 7, no.1), p. 87.

8

Scratched and stunned, they crawled out of the flowered bramble on all fours, laughing. Not being used to all of the attention, I became equally clumsy, nearly hanging myself on low-slung clothes lines or electric wires, cutting my head on the corners of vendors' shacks, and slipping in fresh dog doo, which always seemed to be strategically laid in the middle of the street. I felt very tall and very white.

Seeking a quiet and inconspicuous place, I started walking toward the cathedral bell tower, which jutted above a line of tin roofs near the river. It seemed close. But after several blocks of meandering and a few wrong turns, I found myself in the middle of the Sunday market: two square blocks of patiently swarming men and women with woven bamboo or plastic shopping bags. They deftly avoided stalled fruit carts and mountains of pineapples or mangoes, as they perused hundreds of makeshift wooden stalls in search of a particular item or price. I wandered into the dusty chaos and was swallowed whole, submerged in a writhing labyrinth of color and smell: sizzling chicken feet and bloated sausages skewered on bamboo, huge kettles of boiled duck embryos, plastic buckets full of large black beetles, wooden crates overflowing with okra, eggplant, and seaweed, bananas dangling everywhere in yellow, green, and red clusters, dozens of greasy-hot, bright orange *empanadas* dripping cool on metal racks, and a long row of shiny, steel pails sloshing with silvery milkfish, snails, blue crabs, and shrimp. Nearby a woman hacked off large chunks of a thirty-pound bluefin tuna with a *bolo* (machete), weighed them, and put them in plastic baggies for her customers.

A bit overwhelmed, I wandered into a kind of tunnel, formed by two long walls of bulging hundred-pound sacks of rice, piled high on either side. This emptied into the tobacco section—a row of women who rolled and smoked cigars while waiting for a sale. Walking by, I felt a touch on my leg, and turned back to see an old woman smiling up at me. Squatting with her knees up by her shoulders, she extended to me what looked liked a freshly rolled tobacco leaf, tied at either end with a light string. Then she removed a similar cigar from her own mouth so she could speak. I was astonished. The tip of the cigar that had been inside her mouth was bright orange. She had been smoking with the lit end inside her mouth! She laughed at my surprise.

"Oh, oh…yes, yes. We like better this one inside. Longer lasts," she said. "You try. Free."

I matched her minimal English with my minimal Ilokano (the regional language).

"*Diak kayat ti tobacco, ngem agiaminak.*" ("I don't like tobacco, but thank you.")

Not expecting Ilokano to come out of my mouth, she smiled and motioned for me to sit down. I squatted down in a position similar to hers. Her calm, sparkling eyes were reading me. I knew a little Ilokano. That meant I wasn't a tourist—that I probably wasn't in Laoag on a tarpon fishing expedition or to retrieve my mail-order bride.

She asked my name and where I was from. I reciprocated. "I am Mila," she said. The smile moved to her eyes. She introduced me to some of the other vendors. Then we stopped talking for a while. I squatted there next to her and watched the hot, swirling drama of the market from my less-conspicuous position. Occasionally she would point something out to me—a horse rearing, a vendor arguing with a client, a cart so full of watermelon that it seemed it would topple.

Soon I got a little antsy. I thought I should go. When I told her, she reached behind her basket and picked up a bunch of tiny bananas. She put them in my hands. "Come on Saturday," she said. "We are here."

Then, just before I rose out of my squat, she patted me three times on the knee and nodded assuringly. Her dark, deep-set eyes and soft touch directed me. I heard unspoken words: "Go back into the market. But slow down."

I felt awkward but relieved. Awkward because I relied heavily on spoken words to communicate, but relieved that she didn't, that her eyes knew a language that mine understood, that could somehow transform my eighty-word Ilokano vocabulary into fluency.

I slowly waded back into the market and stopped looking for escape routes. Pulled by the irregular surges of whatever current of people that drew me in, I ducked ropes and bamboo poles as I drifted in a sea of arms and legs and dickering voices. After an hour or so, I found myself washed up by the cathedral, my original destination. I had discovered what I was looking for by not pursuing it, by trusting the human ebb and flow of the market, and a tough-skinned, soft-hearted, fire-eating old woman.

That night I was reading the parable of the sower in preparation for a Bible study I was invited to attend in a nearby village the following week. About a month earlier, when we had visited a nearby province as part of our orientation, I had been asked to help lead a similar discussion. I had begged off due to my newness to the language and culture. Not wanting to offend my host, and unsure how to deal with my unearned privileges, I had attended the discussion with the intent of listening. But several times I was asked for my response. I felt honored to be included but completely unprepared to say anything. I couldn't begin to follow the Ilokano discussion. When I finally did say a few things (in English) to ease the tension (mine), it pushed the conversation to English, a language with which half of those in attendance had little facility. Some eventually stopped talking.

So now I labored through the parable of the sower in my Ilokano Bible, recognizing the story but unable to fully understand it. I switched to an English Bible to translate. Tiring of the selected parable, I read on, and came across the following passage.

Much as you hear, you do not understand; much as you see, you do not perceive. For the heart of this people has grown dull. Their ears hardly hear and their eyes dare not

*see. If they were to see with their eyes, hear with their ears
and understand with their heart, they would turn, and I
would heal them.*

Matthew 13:15

Borrowing from Isaiah, Jesus shares with his disciples
the reason parables are needed in his teaching. He implies
that those who would join his community must learn to see
and hear in radically new ways. I thought of Mila. She seemed
to know this healing language of the heart. That's why she
could communicate so much, yet say so little. And by opening her eyes and ears to an outsider, by *turning* to a stranger,
she was teaching me how to do the same. Her compassionate seeing and hearing enabled me to understand the possibility of my own turning.

For me, the language of the heart which Mila "spoke"
exemplifies the idea of the "Word of God." Rather than lit-
eral words, this metaphorical term refers to religious meaning, to the way God becomes known through human
experience—through relationships and the complex, sometimes torn fabrics of our daily lives. "The deepest level of
communication is not communication but *communion*. It is
wordless," writes Thomas Merton.[3] The Word of God is a
sacred communion with God and other people *for* which we
listen in our everyday lives.[4]

Annie Dillard has also listened for this communion, and
she also connects God's Word with wordlessness, with profound silence: "The silence is all there is. It is the alpha and
the omega....it is the blended note of the ten thousand things,
the whine of wings. You take a step in the right direction to
pray to this silence."[5] Later, alluding to Moses' followers,

---

[3] Quoted in *The Hidden Ground of Love*, William Shannon, editor (New
York: Farrar, Straus, Giroux, 1985), p. x. Italics added.

[4] To listen *for* rather than *to* is important, because "for" suggests a seeking, and perhaps even a co-creation of God's Word, whereas "to" suggests a passive, less creative listening, that the Word is monolithic.

who retreat to their tents in fear when they experience the "Word of God" manifest at Sinai, she advises, "Quit your tents. Pray without ceasing."[6] Dillard implies that a religious life, or a prayerful life, is a life of listening. *Listen* without ceasing.

This listening orientation to prayer and religion, this attempt "to create an opening for God, to invoke God's presence with silence," is key to the idea of *co-mission* across cultures. [7] Co-mission requires that we attempt to create silence in order to discern both the "voice" of the new culture and the "voice" of God.[8] Sometimes neither will speak a language that we can understand. Nevertheless, the missionary persists—patiently, quietly attempting to become radically permeable in relation to both the new culture and to God. There is a simultaneous listening or turning to both.

I sensed this in Mila. Her hospitality, her welcoming, her turning to me, seemed like a kind of prayer, an invocation, a simultaneous turning or opening to God—a communion. She hears and speaks the language of the heart, hears and does God's grace-filled Word. She turns hearts with her listening heart. From this perspective, *she* is the missionary.

Essential to the deconstruction of lingering, harmful mission stereotypes in the U.S., is recognizing that missionaries need not be white, English-speaking, college-degreed, Christian, straight, from an economically privileged country (such as the U.S.), or an "expert" in anything. They are simply people who attempt to hear and do God's Word. The integrity of the co-mission is not tied to project development or completion, but to how fully the missionary can open her-

---

[5] Annie Dillard, *Teaching a Stone to Talk* (New York: Harper and Collins, 1982), p. 94.

[6] Ibid.

[7] Perry Lefevre, "The Right Word," *CTS Tower News* (Spring, 1988), p. 4.

[8] For a more complete definition of mission vs. co-mission and of the relationship between cross-cultural mission and cross-cultural education, see the Afterword.

self or himself to the new culture and to God's Word—to the possibility of communion.

My encounter with Mila applied to the above scripture passage invites a new interpretation for One-Third World readers. In the historical context of cross-cultural mission, or other so-called "development," the One-Third World has sometimes viewed the Two-Thirds World as the dull-hearted "they" that the gospel writer mentions, the objectified, "uneducated" masses who need to be "turned" to our definitions of "God" and "civilization." Those of us in the One-Third World who hope to co-mission, who hope to mutually hear and do God's Word with our Two-Thirds World partners (whether in a foreign country or our own), will need to acknowledge that "we" are part of the "they." We go to the Two-Thirds World not to turn anyone, but to learn how to be turned ourselves.

Do not depend on the hope of results....the big results are not in your hands or mine....they suddenly happen and we can share in them; but there is no point in building our lives on this personal satisfaction, which may be denied us and which after all is not that important....In the end it is the reality of personal relationships that saves everything.

Thomas Merton[1]

From Sower to Soil:
Turned Upside Down by God's Word

erton's advice to a young political activist may also be instructive for missionaries, or for any who believe that they can determine "the results," and that the "success" of their work manifests their belief in God and God's belief in them. Missionaries and mission boards were originally preoccupied with results: new converts, new churches, new schools, new clinics. These were visible, measurable proof of success in their mission *to* the new culture. Merton suggests a different focus: that our task as missionaries (and as *human* beings), is not to impose, but to share—both the

---

[1]This often-excerpted quote comes from Thomas Merton's 2/15/66 letter to Jim Forest. The entire letter is included in *The Hidden Ground of Love*, William Shannon, editor (New York: Farrar, Straus, Giroux, 1985), pp. 294-295.

risks and the joys of the host culture—to realize that "human relationships save everything." If we believe this, if we can listen and see compassionately enough to try and build a bridge of understanding *with* our partners in the host culture, if we are able to turn to them, then perhaps we will share in the "big results." But if there is nothing we perceive as measurable results, the attempted bridge building, the turning, the mutual risk will still be valuable in itself.

+ + +

I did attend the Bible study in a nearby village the following week. We discussed the parable of the sower, Mark's version. We sat in a circle, gathering around the story. Most sat on chairs or the sofa, others squatted, or stood nearby. The home consisted of two large cement rooms and two makeshift interior "walls": a movable wood divider, which framed in a sleeping area, and a large hanging blanket, behind which two women prepared *pancit* and a cool drink for *merienda*. It was hot. Two small dogs slept inside the circle on the cool cement floor. A young child roamed from person to person looking for attention and relief from the heat. Pastor Luna opened with a prayer and then read the passage to begin the discussion.

> *Listen! The sower went out to sow. As he sowed, some of the seed fell along a path and the birds came and ate it up. Some of the seed fell on rocky ground where it had little soil, and sprang up immediately because it had no depth; but when the sun rose and burned it, it withered because it had no roots. Other seed fell among thorn bushes, and the thorns grew and choked it, so it didn't produce any grain. But some seed fell on good soil, grew up and increased and yielded grain; some produced thirty times as much, others sixty and others one hundred times as much. And Jesus added, "Listen then, if you have ears."*
>
> Mark 4:3–9

After a long silence Pastor Luna initiated the discussion. He asked us to try to first read the story from the point of view of a rice farmer.

"Though most Bible study leaders would focus their interpretation on the soil as the problem, a rice farmer would rather look at the *sower* as the problem. From his point of view a responsible farmer would not just randomly scatter seeds like the sower in the parable. Rather, he or she would first work to prepare the soil. This means he would have to plow and harrow the soil carefully to soften the ground. He would have to at least try and remove the stones, the weeds, and the thorns, before planting the seed. In other words, *the sower would have to take the soil seriously.* From this point of view the problem is not with the quality of soil, but with the quality of sower. The rice farmer knows from experience that he (a sower) is educated by the soil and dependent upon it. It is where new life comes from! It is his sustenance. The same is true for pastors and church leaders. They must be deeply rooted in the soil, in their community."

Mr. Coloma, a retired teacher, responded next, also adapting the parable to the Philippine context. He was less metaphorical. "Yes, but the rice farmer also knows that there is very little good soil left. When God was talking to Adam and Eve he said, 'Take care of this.' He didn't say, 'Here, all of this is yours. Do whatever you want with it.' But that's what we've done. The illegal loggers and mining companies have stripped our mountains and much of the good soil has washed away. Some of the slash and burn farmers have had the same effect. If there is any good soil, it's the big companies that own it—some of the same ones that are destroying it. They grow wealthy but don't leave us much. If we can find a piece of land it is likely to be rocky or full of weeds. But few farmers could even afford that, let alone the seed."

Jenalyn, a college student, had a different view. "But this story is about spreading the gospel, not agrarian reform. Jesus is saying that we must plant the seeds of God that others have planted in us. We must tell the story. If we believe, if we have God's word, then we have the seed. We can sow."

Pastor Luna synthesized. "I think both of you have a point. We need bread both for our souls and our bodies if we are to survive. We know that if we cannot buy or grow enough rice for our families, if they are hungry or ill, if we cannot sustain them physically, then we are less able to sow God's word, to spread the gospel. During these times, when we're hard up, perhaps we don't even feel like sowers but more like the rocky, weedy soil, unable to fully receive God's message. Yet it is also during these times of suffering, of want, of thirst and hunger, that we must survive only on God's spirit, on our faith.

"There are also times where we may choose to suffer or take risks—in the struggle for justice. During these times, we may lack the physical sustenance we need, but we are able to sow the seed because the powerful spirit of God's love sustains us in the struggle. We have faith that God will protect and nurture us. Perhaps the important thing is that our struggle or our suffering has meaning, that it is not in vain. If we believe this, then perhaps it is possible to continue to sow, to continue to struggle toward God's kingdom."

While listening to the discussion, I considered the biblical context for the original Markan community. What did members of the Jesus movement think when they sat around discussing this story in the first century? Jesus was dead and could no longer rally the forces. His followers were being brutally persecuted. The Jewish sects they had thought would join their movement hadn't, so it had become fragmented. At the time, to be a follower of Jesus, to have faith, required great courage. Faith equaled courage. In that context the message would seem to be just keep sowing the seeds. Despite the persecution, despite the hunger, despite the fear, despite the poverty, just keep sowing the word of God, the word of justice. Don't worry whether it takes. Don't depend on the hope of results. Most of the soil is not fertile, not capable of receiving the radical message of God's kingdom, but this faith, this struggle, is not about numbers. The writer frames the parable with a plea to listen. But it was/is a difficult message to hear.

I knew of many people in the circle around me whose faith did equal courage. Some had struggled to free political detainees and assisted victims of the political repression that surrounded the war. Others had fought with tribal Filipinos to protect their land and culture from being destroyed by foreign developers. Still others were working long hours as pastors of isolated churches for little or no money. Their faith caused them to risk.

I also knew that most of the people around me lived a life of material subsistence. They had shelter, clothing, and enough food, but not much more, sometimes less. Coming from a country that espoused satiation, I perceived them as "living on the edge." But I was beginning to realize that it was not necessarily the edge of despair, or failure, or hopelessness. Perhaps it was the edge of God's reign. Like everyone, they needed money and material goods to sustain themselves. I do not want to romanticize or trivialize poverty. But a number of the people in the circle did *know,* with their very lives, that they did not need money to buy the seeds God wanted them to sow, any more than Jesus' followers did in the first century. And I wondered if this didn't grant them, like God, the capacity to create something out of nothing—or at least to do a great deal with very little.

Faith has rarely equaled or catalyzed courage in my life. Occasionally there have been sowers, like Pastor Luna, who have reminded me that we can't buy the seeds God wants us to sow, who have inspired me to take risks, to go beyond my spiritual and physical limitations. This has happened in the Philippines, Guatemala, Nicaragua, Appalachia, on the south side of Chicago, on the Rosebud and Pine Ridge Reservations in South Dakota, and other places. Other One-Third World Christians who have lived and worked in the Two-Thirds World, who have taken part in "mission" work camps, in an "urban plunge," in sister-church or human rights delegations to other countries/cultures, know that these experiences can be life-changing. But it can also be difficult to translate these profoundly spiritual experiences back to our everyday lives, to sustain and integrate them, to continue to risk. We sometimes return to long periods of complacency, longing for the challenge, the inspiration of the other culture.

During these times perhaps we should remember that many of these people, in these cultures of subsistence and struggle, gather around the same story that we do. Perhaps their mission to us is to teach us how to become the soil in our own gardens, in our own contexts, to help move us from being rocky, weedy soil, from a preoccupation with material security or satiation, to fertile soil, to a risking life, where faith can equal courage, where we can receive and nurture God's prophetic seeds.

The question is, Will we let these sowers, these missionaries, these "foreigners," these strangers, cultivate us, *turn us upside down*, open us to a new culture, to a new Word from God, and even to a new mission? This cannot happen if we still believe at some level that the role of the missionary is to "tell the story to the nations" and "turn their hearts to the right." Though One-Third World missionaries sent from contexts of economic privilege may have important gifts to share in the new cultures, our orientation, as outsiders, as guests, (and in some cases as descendants of former colonizers) should be that of soil rather than sower. There may be an opportunity for preparing the soil or sowing later, after we return to our culture of origin, whether that be across the city or across the ocean.

Attentiveness without an aim is the
supreme form of prayer.

Simone Weil[1]

Dancing Geckos

The slow pace of my acculturation in Laoag resulted in a daily life full of misperception and miscommunication. I laughed when I should have been looking serious and concerned. I looked serious and concerned when I should have been laughing. I closed doors that should have been left open. I had answers to questions that no one asked. In my naiveté, I was often painfully (for others) direct and honest. I was drowning in a sea of languages. Some were verbal. I was disappointed that people didn't use the phrases or pronunciations I had learned in language school, or that they wanted to practice their broken English with a native speaker, rather than struggle with our broken Ilokano. The college had furnished an overly large, dark, cement and

---

[1]Quoted in Bonzanic, "Patience," *Manoa*, p. 88.

wood house, with little furniture and bars over all the windows. When we suggested that it was too big for two people, we were hushed with knowing smiles. But as was so often the case, we didn't know what they knew. A few days later our respective deans, with big, understanding smiles, gave us each what seemed like a heavy teaching load (five classes, five preparations). There were few books or audiovisual aids. Much of the time there was no electricity. We had to bring our own chalk and erasers. The classrooms were large and noisy. It was hot.

Eventually another teacher and four students moved in with us, and we realized that the house was not too big, but just right. We also discovered that we *did* have a light teaching load, as many of our colleagues taught seven or even eight classes. We learned how to teach with few books and occasional electricity. We learned more about language, the nonverbal kind. And we became more patient spectacles, less flustered by our undesired celebrity status.

The clusters of children that buzzed around me on the way to school still made me uneasy, but only because their perpetual pointing, laughing, and staring reminded me that I was a permanent outsider. The ironic thing was that while I wanted to be an "insider," to be accepted and included, to get beyond cordiality, I simultaneously longed for a U.S. brand of privacy, for a place to hide. As I became more consumed by these competing desires, I tried to remember Mila's unspoken words in the market.

I slowed down and waded in. I tried to talk with *bagoong* or *bibingka* vendors in my mangled Ilokano. I asked a rice farmer to show me how to plant seedlings. Though underqualified, I agreed to teach a guitar class at the college. There were eleven students and three guitars. One guitar stayed in tune. We still made music. I stopped avoiding the children. My frustration evolved into curiosity. What did they think of the lanky *puraw* who walked twice as fast as everyone else? Could they tell that I didn't always know where I was going or what I would say or do when I arrived? What did they suspect? What did they see? We watched each other, and we both wondered what *the other* saw.

I watched a sea of black-haired kids suck mango seeds white, stick-tease rats and chickens, fall asleep in the *jeepney*, rock-flatten bottle caps, float sandals in the sewer, lie down on the backs of enormous *carabao*, dangle from the *balete* tree, play basketball barefoot on the hot, cracked cement, buy warm, brown paper sacks of *pan de sal* at dawn at the bakery, and hug them all the way home to their mothers.

I began to understand their curiosity as an invitation to participate in their culture. I knew that if I was going to be *turned*, I would need to become more like them: to wonder and wander on purpose, to ask more questions, to live wholly in the present tense, to depend on others without regret or a feeling of weakness. Like so many of my other Filipino mentors, the children reminded me that I would best adapt to Ilokano culture not by trying to "help," but by sharing my cross-cultural ignorance.

"At every margin or boundary there is the possibility of confrontation with the vulnerability, ignorance, discomfort or fear to be found not only in the situation or in a protagonist, but in *ourselves*," writes Anthony Gittins.[2] The children were teaching me a central tenet of cross-cultural co-mission: *vulnerability is not weakness*.

+ + +

One morning I went over to the college for my usual ten o'clock class and discovered that morning classes were canceled. This had happened before. Sometimes I knew why; sometimes I didn't. With the gift of a free morning, and a bit frustrated by the seeming randomness of our daily lives, I decided to make a list of things to accomplish that day. Overly intent on my blank notepad, I didn't notice a battalion of red ants that had rerouted its march across my desk in search of

---

[2]Anthony Gittins, *Gifts and Strangers: Meeting the Challenge of Inculturation* (New York: Paulist Press, 1989), p. 140. Italics added.

a cracker and smear of peanut butter beneath my papers. A sharp bite brought me back to the present moment. I cleaned the mess up and wiped off the ants but then noticed more on the window sill—dozens of disordered ant platoons obsessively marching toward who knows what. They constantly bumped into each other and knocked each other out of the way without apology or pause. One large one knocked a piece of bread out of the jaws of a smaller one. Neither stopped moving. Many literally walked on the backs of others in order to get to wherever they were going more quickly. They frequently reversed direction without reason or warning—movement without meaning, busyness as virtue. I decided these ants were from Chicago, my home. They belonged on Michigan Avenue at rush hour—thousands of arms and legs propelling determined, yet oblivious bodies toward unknown destinations.

I stopped my list of "things to do" and looked beyond the ants out the window. A scraggly, tailless, yellow cat had crawled on an adjacent window sill, apparently stalking something on the roof just below us. I looked closer. The cat was watching a large lizard, which was watching a large cockroach, which sensing the lizard suddenly set off in a menacing waddle and disappeared over the edge of the roof. The lizard followed. The cat didn't. At that moment I turned to see if anyone was watching me. Convinced that no one was, I started on my list.

- cross-cult. education report
- scrub out water tank
- pick up new gas tank for stove
- market: fruit, okra, coffee, fish, *bagoong*, rice
- Xerox articles for classes

The first task was to write an essay analyzing the "challenges of a cross-cultural educator" for an education journal in the U.S. I plugged in the typewriter. There was no electricity. That was the first challenge. I dug out a legal pad and pencil and began to scratch out some ideas.

*Initially, the central challenge of teaching in a radically differ-
ent culture is accepting the fact that you are much more student
than teacher. The challenge is not to "teach the material" but to
learn how to open yourself to the ways the students can teach you
about their culture and about how to teach in their culture. This
requires paying compassionate attention.*

Too vague. The editors wanted concrete anecdotes that
could serve as cross-cultural parables about teaching. I
started over. A few minutes later I was interrupted by some
giggling outside the window. Rene and Gin, two little neighbor girls, were squatting on the same rusted orange corrugated roof from which the cockroach had just escaped. They
were giggling because they had decided to pull down their
shorts and have an early morning pee right there on the roof.
One got the definite feeling that they knew they weren't supposed to do this, and that if their grandfather found out (he
was chopping wood in front of the house), they would be
in big trouble. But in the meantime they were delighted,
laughing and pointing at their streams of urine, which
slowly ran down the metal valleys and over the edge of the
roof. They then scrambled up to the edge and shrieked as
they watched a couple of extremely perplexed turkeys receive an unusual shower. I heard myself laughing nearly as
loudly as the girls.

Back to my assignment. Another attempt:

*Many of my students arrive in Laoag after a day or two of
jeepney and bus travel from their tribal communities in the
mountains. They bring hundred-pound sacks of rice on their backs
to sustain them for the fifteen-week term. Some bring chickens and
cabbages and coconuts. One student told me he was living on rice,
marunggay fruit (they had a tree behind his boarding house), and
two cans of sardines a week. He wasn't complaining, though. He
had invited me for lunch and wanted to "warn" me about what
we'd be having. This student, like some others I knew, viewed each
class, each hour in school, as a gift, as a possibility. He had to assume*

this present tense orientation because he was never sure how long he would be in college—another week, another month, another quarter? It depended on his aunt, who was a domestic worker in Hong Kong. She sent the tuition for the first term, but not for the second. He left for Manila to try and find work. He couldn't, so returned to his home province, to subsistence farming with his father—an increasingly difficult life.

At the college where I teach in the states my students are mostly middle class. Most always knew they would go to college. It's a given, a necessary hoop. Campus issues often concern parking policies and computer accessibility. Many students struggle financially, but few with day-to-day survival. Most find the cost of a community college affordable. They can think more long term.

I wasn't satisfied with this either. It was oversimplified. My students in the U.S. struggle too, but in different ways. Many have been recently downsized out of jobs. What's "middle class" anymore? I haven't the slightest idea. I was getting frustrated.

I looked up to see two geckos shaking the screen in their endless frenzies to go nowhere. Like the ants, their movement seemed pointless, accomplishing nothing, a life reduced to a few thousand push-button scrambles. They'd dart to the rusty perimeter, then return to non-rest. They'd flypaper-tongue a mosquito, contemplate a patched hole, fail to squeeze through a crack, then return to nervous pause.

Sometimes I felt like a gecko in Laoag. I had tremendous energy and desire to move, and I did. I was busy, but it all seemed meaningless. During one of these frustrating periods I remember reading Masao Takenaka's *God is Rice*. He helped me better understand the limits of modern "Western" culture.

We live an increasingly hectic life and we are busy with much busyness. The character for "busy" in Chinese writing, which Koreans and Japanese also use, literally means "to destroy one's heart." If we are too busy we forget what

is most important. It is interesting that the same compo-
nents of the character for busy are used to indicate forget-
fulness. Both mean the destruction of one's heart.[3]

When we are "busy" completing our list of tasks, we forget to pay attention to things that matter. Our heart may be
destroyed or unable to *turn* due to our preoccupation, our
inner drive to control time and life.

Ironically, I had perceived the opportunity to go to the
Philippines in part as a chance to live "out of control" or
with someone else in control, who wouldn't and couldn't
expect too much from me, precisely because I didn't fit in.
Though this is perhaps not a traditional "missionary" orientation, in retrospect I think it was a good one. It was my way
of losing my life in order to find it.

But when we arrived, I found adapting to Ilokano culture was often less difficult than the simultaneous process of
coming to terms with ingrained U.S. culture. Despite my best
intentions, when I arrived in Laoag I immediately sought
responsibility, a role, a means of self-definition—tasks to keep
me busy, which I could somehow use to measure my success
or failure.

Takenaka reminded me that the cross-cultural education
process continues whether we want it to or not, whether we
are "busy" or not. "Meaning" is not easily measured, and it
may come to us most readily in the times when we are least
busy. "Being" may be more important than "doing" in the
new culture. Some doing might come later, or it might not.
The meaning of the cross-cultural education or the co-mission might reveal itself in the future tense, but only if we pay
attention and risk vulnerability in the now, in the present.

What am I supposed to do here? What is my role? How
will my skills fit in? What will I accomplish? How will I know
if I'm successful? These were the questions that cluttered my
mind during the first few months in Laoag.

---

[3]Masao Takenaka, *God is Rice:Asian Culture and Faith* (Geneva: World
Council of Churches, 1986), p. 8.

I later found a different set of questions to be more helpful: Am I listening? What do I hear? How can I listen more carefully? Am I watching? What do I see? How can I see more carefully? Am I turnable? What does turning feel like?

I kept watching the geckos, their entropic dashing, their delicate chaos. I blocked out the lure of the notepad and focused. Slowly, over the next hour, I began to notice redundant movements and pauses. These evolved into several patterns which slowly became clear, even obvious. By noon, a crawling intricacy, a prehistoric choreography, a short-circuited waltz, had revealed itself in an unending string of cold-blooded encores. They continued despite my silent ovations, and long after I left for my one o'clock class.

BEYOND THE WHITE NOISE

II

When his [the missionary's] house or his chapel is stoned by men who do not understand him he gets the same thrill that came to our fathers from the war whoop off in the forest....

Bruce Kirshner,[1] Disciples of Christ missionary to the Philippines (1905-1917)

Charity wounds [the one] who receives, and our whole moral effort is directed towards suppressing the unconscious harmful patronage of a rich almoner.

Marcel Mauss[2]

White Noise

The journey to Mamalao took two days. After a three-hour bus trip from Manila south to Batangas, Carol and I boarded a rusty, overloaded ferry. It bobbed and weaved through choppy waters for four hours before arriving in Calapan, the Mindoro port. There we were met by Modesto, a community organizer who worked in Mamalao and who would accompany us the next day on the final leg of the journey. As we boarded a tricycle that would take us into town, he explained that the people of Mindoro were known as the *Mangyans,* and that the twelve families who lived in Mamalao, the village we would be visiting, belonged to a tribal group within the Mangyans, known as the *Irayans.*

---

[1]Clymer, *Protestant Missionaries in the Philippines,* p. 22. Brackets added.
[2]Marcel Mauss as quoted in Gittins, *Gifts and Strangers,* p. 91

Modesto found us a plate of rice and squid for dinner and a bunk at a friend's house for the night. About midnight we woke to the high-pitched squeaks and grinding teeth of a pack of large rats feeding on a rice sack a few feet from our heads. I turned on the lights, the rats scattered, and I dragged the sack into the next room. When I turned the lights off the rats again swarmed on the rice. I tried to sleep, but instead, like a child, found myself listening for monsters. Soon I heard them. I looked up to see the shining eyes of another cadre of rats marching over us on a ceiling rafter. Terrified that one would slip and land angry and wild-eyed on my chest, I pulled my *malong* over my head and turned the fan on high to help drown out the menacing squeaks. Nothing helped. One by one the minutes blinked by on my digital wristwatch.

Eventually, morning came. After some more rice and dried fish for breakfast, I loaded my backpack. Unsure of what to expect, and consumed by a delusionary belief in my self-sufficiency, I packed a mini-pharmacy, mosquito netting, and three changes of clothes.

The journey to Mamalao was part of an ongoing orientation program, one of a series of week-long visits, or "exposures" we made at various times throughout our appointment to help us better understand the cultural and socio-political diversity of the islands. Even though the orientation materials challenged us to "identify" with the communities we visited, I wondered if that were really possible. Could we genuinely associate or feel anything the community felt in just seven days? Mamalao seemed so physically and culturally distant to me that my imaginative expectations continually drifted to the exotic. It would be easy to romanticize this new world and therefore believe the orientation material—that I was capable of "risky identification."

When I realized we had left our rain ponchos in Manila, I started to worry. It was typhoon season. I went looking for Modesto. He soon returned from the market with a large bag of rice, a small jar of instant coffee, and three cans of sardines. He also had bought several huge plastic bags, which worked better than my poncho, slipping easily over both my body and backpack. How had he known?

Not wanting to sleep with the rats again, I was glad to leave for Mamalao. But I also knew that Mauro's friends had given us the best bed in the house (a four-by-six-foot wooden frame) and the only fan. They had thumbtacked a sheet over the open doorway for privacy. The other four or five people who lived there had all piled into a small room above us. They had offered Carol and me, complete strangers, the very best they had, but I had yielded to my fear rather than to their hospitality.

A driver pulled up in a muddy, rusted jeep. We climbed in and headed for the foothills. When the road ended, we crawled out and began the half-day hike up the mountain to the village. Modesto had packed only a towel with a few clothes wrapped inside. He stuffed this in a plastic bag with a small, aluminum rice pot. He also carried our food up the mountain.

An hour into the hike the rains came. In minutes the steep path became a reddish-brown water slide which Modesto miraculously negotiated in his rubber flip-flops. I slogged and slipped after him in my mud-packed Nike running shoes, pausing every few minutes to pick off the leeches which suddenly appeared on my ankles, arms, and every leaf or vine I grasped for support.

We finally reached the village and stopped in a small bamboo chapel to rest. The rain was booming on the metal roof. We had to yell to hear each other. Modesto smiled and pointed to the roof.

"White man's noise," he said.

Thinking he meant "white noise," I nodded. The hammering rain on the metal buried any sounds from the jungle. The buzzing insects, whistling birds, and screeching monkeys were all drowned out by the white noise. But for me there was something about the all-consuming noise that was comforting, that created a kind of placelessness and time-lessness that allowed me to turn inward for a moment, to escape the reality of my isolation, my "exposure," my not fitting in, my whiteness.

Modesto later explained that a white missionary had bought the chapel roof as a gift when he visited the community several years ago, which was why Modesto called the engulfing sound of rain on steel "white man's noise." The white man had left a noisy roof. Modesto didn't mean the term critically, or to suggest that the twelve families who lived in Mamalao were ungrateful for the shiny metal roof. Many were actually proud of it, proud that they had carried the roof piece by piece to such an isolated place in the mountains.

Given the choice, though, the people of Mamalao might have spent the money differently, perhaps for rice seedlings to plant on the terraces they had just started on the mountain. Roofs were something they could easily construct themselves from bamboo or other local fronds. Thatched roofs didn't last as long as the metal roofs, but they were cooler and more easily repaired. Not to mention quieter.

The rain continued. That night, while lying next to Modesto on the floor of our bamboo hut, I considered the drawbacks of the metal roof. Not just the monetary cost but all that it silenced during the rainy season—the voices from the mountain. A good-hearted outsider had unknowingly misread the culture in an attempt to help. I knew that I did the same thing in Laoag. I seldom knew for sure what to give or how to receive, or what I had *already* given and received. Because even though I could easily distinguish between the sound of rain on metal and the sound of rain on thatch, even though I could discern the obvious, stark differences between our cultures, the torrent on our thatched roof also seemed like white noise to me, a blur of water sounds.

Modesto heard more. Beyond our open windows and the blowing sheets of rain on our thatched roof, he heard a *carabao* sloshing toward home, a bamboo tree slapping the sides of our hut, frayed banana leaves flapping in the wind, a rat grinding a stray rice grain in a rafter above us, a gecko coughing just outside our door, the high-pitched whine of a bat darting by our window. And he knew that Fely, our neighbor, had just cut a new slat for his planting sled with his machete and was now tapping on our door. Fely had brought us a freshly roasted cassava as a gift to welcome "the visitors." He wrapped it tightly in a banana leaf to protect it from the rain and keep it warm.

We were out of sardines by the second day. We still had plenty of rice, but that was it. When we had left Calapan, I had wondered how three small cans of sardines would sustain us for the week. "Well, rice it is," I decided. There were only four more days.

That evening, Modesto took his machete and walked out into the nearby jungle. *"Mangan tayon"* ("Let's eat"), he said before he left, smiling. Since he was a Tagalog speaker from Luzon, this was the only Ilokano phrase he knew. He used it often to tease me, implying I was always hungry. He returned a few minutes later sopping wet, cradling an enormous jackfruit, a large banana heart, three mangoes, and a coconut scraper he had borrowed from Fely. By candlelight he cracked a coconut, separated the meat, grated it, put that in a bowl, and added water. Then he quartered the jackfruit with the machete and diced two of the quarters into small pieces. He sliced the banana heart finely, like an onion. Knowing that I would be more comfortable with a task, he asked me to make the fire and cook the rice.

After wringing out the coconut milk from the shavings, Modesto poured it over the sliced jackfruit and banana heart. He simmered this over the fire as our *sida* (topping) for the rice. Then he disappeared again with the machete. He returned with two large banana leaves, our place mats. Sitting on the bamboo floor, we ate the jackfruit and banana heart over rice with our fingers. We had mangoes for dessert. This was one of many meals Modesto would quickly gather from the jungle and then prepare, with only a machete, a small pan, and a little oil.

The third day in Mamalao, Modesto took me along to visit some of the families. Their bamboo huts were set on stilts. We climbed four steps up a bamboo ladder to visit a young mother, Nita, who nursed her baby while playing with two other children on the woven bamboo floor of a small room. The ceiling was low, about four feet, so we squatted, folding our bodies in thirds. Nita looked down when we greeted her, then talked to Modesto in hushed tones in the corner, looking off into the trees, never smiling.

At that moment, while both watching and pretending not to watch Nita and Modesto, I realized that I was not the only one on an "exposure." The host community shared in the vulnerability as well. Perhaps we could identify with each other after all.

If so, our identification was much more personal than political. I felt great sympathy for the community's ongoing struggle against the Japanese marble mining corporation that was tearing up their mountain and threatening to contaminate their spring (the only available source of clean water). We sat up until midnight one evening listening to the elders strategize about how to deal with these outsiders, how to protect themselves, how to survive.

I lamented the tragedy, the seemingly inevitable destruction of their now-fragile culture. I felt their frustration toward the multinational corporations and the lowlanders in Mindoro who refused to recognize their tribal law of ancestral domain, by which the land was theirs because they had always worked it.

But perhaps because I was an outsider and am historically linked to the One-Third World's conquest of underdeveloped countries (a conquest this Japanese company continued), the most profound "identification" I felt with the Irayan people was the shared social vulnerability which I experienced that day sitting on the floor of Nita's hut.

She felt both obligated to welcome me and extremely uncomfortable. I couldn't speak Tagalog or their tribal tongue, and she didn't know any Ilokano (the regional language I had studied) or much English. We both felt exposed and unsure.

Thankfully, soon after our arrival at her hut, the rain came, and I felt myself pulling away, slipping into the comforting white noise, the soft wet drum on the thatch. Just then one of her children ran up to me, grabbed my beard, and gave it a twist. It hurt, and Modesto and Nita saw my anguish. We all laughed, the woman and I mostly out of relief. The child, exposed to something new as well, a white man with a beard, had brought us together by literally pulling me out of the comforting white noise and into conversation. Unknowingly, he had created a tiny opening in the wall of ignorance and fear that separated us, reminding me I was choosing to hear only white noise.

A fire and roasting cassava on the ground beneath us filled the room with smoke and the prospect of lunch. Since I had already been in many situations where Filipinos offered me nearly everything they had to eat, seemingly choosing hospitality over their own long-term nutrition, I was unsure whether we should stay and consume Nita's precious cassavas. Finally, at my urging, Modesto declined her offer. We thanked her and got ready to leave.

I think my confusion was due to my inability to let go of my North American concept of hospitality, the product of a "culture of accumulation," which views the amassment of material goods as the primary measure of success. Modesto knew I was mistaken, but in his own hospitality, he deferred, not wanting to confront or offend me.

I wasn't really listening to Nita, to Modesto, or to the culture. I didn't yet understand the possibility of hospitality in a "culture of distribution."[3] It would have been immoral for Nita not to feed and welcome a stranger, a vulnerable

---

[3] This parallel set of socioeconomic philosophies (cultures of accumulation and distribution) is useful in understanding the difference between the One-Third and Two-Thirds Worlds.

outsider, in a context where food was difficult to come by. In a culture of distribution, the community is morally obligated to provide sustenance for all, not satiation for a few. In her hospitality, Nita was offering me that communal right. For her, the shame associated with inhospitality was much worse than hunger.

As we stood to leave, Nita lifted her hand toward Modesto, said "No," in English, then something in Tagalog. After she finished Modesto turned to me. "We stay," he said.

It was then that Nita looked at me for the first time. Her eyes, lifting questions, interrogated, then softened. She gave each of us several small, hot pieces of cassava. During the next half-hour, as we ate, she tried to say a few words in English and I a few in Tagalog. I was listening so hard that I completely forgot it was raining.

Another Mission Roof

The Sunday after we returned to Laoag we were invited to participate in a nearby church's elementary school graduation program. The village was a three-hour jeepney ride away. We were graciously received with warm hospitality and given what seemed to be an unearned elevated status. This was not uncommon.

Though our Ilokano was poor, we received some help with translation beforehand, and we gave our little talks in the dialect. We pronounced the phrases adequately, though we only knew what we were saying about half the time. The community seemed surprised and appreciative of our efforts. Even though good pronunciation in no way suggests mastery of a language, we allowed ourselves this misleading pleasure, the illusory assurance that we were acculturating rapidly.

Perhaps we needed to pretend because we were often confused, wondering more about how we were being perceived by our host community than how to perceive the onslaught of vastly different cultural cues. We graciously devoured affirmation and feedback of any kind, anything that might suggest how to better fit in in Ilocos.

After the ceremony, as we were moving toward the pot-luck tables laden with *chicken adobo, pinakbet,* and *pancit,* a woman came up to us and started talking about our leaving a big "Christmas present." This was in March.

"We really need a new roof," she said. She then listed all of the other missionaries who had visited over the last ten years or so and the monetary donations they had made. A pastor in Hawaii had raised enough money with his congregation to build an entire church in a nearby village. Another one in Ohio still sends one hundred dollars a year, even though he hasn't been back to the Philippines since the fifties.

A few minutes later, several other people approached, smiling, shaking our hands, and making vague comments about the roof in a mix of Ilokano and English which I couldn't fully understand. Finally, we were presented with an envelope with our name typed on it.

"Anything you can do is fine," one of the women assured us. But some of the people, probably thinking we had a large, accessible checking account, appeared to be waiting for us to make the donation which would buy the shiny, new, cor-rugated metal roof.

Launching into an explanation, I said we were on a Phil-ippine salary (about $250 U.S. per month) which was estab-lished by the United Church of Christ in the Philippines (the U.C.C.P., their denomination). We were given specific guide-lines by the U.C.C.P. not to access outside resources to fund special projects. This attempt to live a more Philippine lifestyle was supposed to help prevent missionaries from insulating themselves from the community and culture; to prevent microwaves, televisions, VCRs, and cars next door to wood-burning stoves, broken radios, and homemade bicycles. We were no longer called missionaries, but "cowork-ers," to suggest a more egalitarian approach to international mission. The U.C.C.P. developed this new approach to es-cape the tangle of paternalistic strings which foreign mission boards and some missionaries kept (and keep) tied to their funding and political position in the host country.

Immediately after I had explained most of this, one of the women asked if I wanted more *adobo*. I decided I did. I smiled, looked stupid, and slipped two hundred pesos (about eight dollars) into the designated envelope. Naively believing that most of the women and men hovering around us had not seen the exact amount (a generous contribution by Philippine standards, but measly by U.S. standards), I carefully sealed the envelope. We hoped they wouldn't open it until we left, after we were safely squashed in a jeepney and bouncing toward Laoag.

Just before we left, I noticed that Mang Laurento, one of the pastors, looked a bit uncomfortable. While shaking hands and saying good-bye, he told us that he hoped we hadn't taken the roof request the wrong way. He said they really hadn't known the U.C.C.P. policy. He thought it was good. "We want you to eat what we eat. We want you to learn how we live," he said. "That's how it should be."

His words, "We want you learn how we live," hung in my head for days, like laundry in the rainy season, perpetually damp, forever dripping, unfinished. I finally realized the inherent hypocrisy in the lengthy explanation of "mission as partnership" that I had given to him and others in the community that day.

My method had completely contradicted my message. My explanation, my telling our hosts how *their* church defined mission, was an overtly North American response to the new-roof issue. Though my ideas were "politically correct" in content and my tone conciliatory, I had still assumed control. I had done all of the talking, expected the community to adapt to my interpretation, and then got out of there as fast as I could.

Fearing that I would be forced into the old missionary model, I had actually assumed it, completely ignoring the Philippine context. I should have taken the hint when the woman offered me more *adobo* and provided a subtle option out of the pending confrontation. I should have defused the conflict through a third party, allowing those requesting the roof to save face. I should have joked that I had forgotten my checkbook and then explained privately to Mang Laurento about our limited resources and the new mission policies. I shouldn't have been in such a hurry to get back to Laoag. I should have waited and listened longer.

The whole experience made me think about the community in Mamalao, which had received a new mission roof they did not ask for and would not have chosen. Perhaps the ironic juxtaposition of these two experiences, of these two roofs, suggests the complexity of evolving cross-cultural relationships between the One-Third and Two-Thirds Worlds. Both "worlds" need to relearn how to give and receive the gifts of their cultures. In one case, a North American missionary freely gives a roof, a material gift, to "help" an isolated tribal Filipino community. But it is not the kind of help they want or need. In the second case, a Filipino community asks for a material gift, a roof, from North American missionaries, assuming that this is the easiest and/or best way for them to give or help.

Perhaps the point is that communities in both the One-Third and Two-Thirds Worlds need help and have gifts. Both need liberation. Mang Laurento and the community in Mamalao remind us that one key to achieving this mutual liberation, one key to struggling with the Two-Thirds World toward partnership, is for us in the One-Third World to learn how to wait and listen. This is perhaps the greatest gift we can give.

Waiting and listening are necessary if we are to learn how to receive the gifts of our partner cultures. But if they don't speak, or if we don't hear the voices, it may mean patiently listening to silence. Silence does not imply that there are no voices, no music, no culture. As any good percussionist knows, silence and sound are equally important. The silence is *part* of the rhythm, of the music, of the culture, of the history. It has profound meaning. If we wait long enough and listen hard enough, we will gain the capacity to hear new voices emerge from our white noise. Voices which have always been there. Voices full of new rhythms and melodies. Voices which create history and new hope.

*Just before the rain falls into sound,
that's when we promise ourselves to
really live.*

Stephanie Marlis[1]

The Rain
Makes
the Roof
Sing

T yphoon Kadiang arrived abruptly, taking down tree limbs and power lines, blowing rain through the screens, cooling the house. When we lost electricity I lit a small candle and anchored it on a metal lid with a few drops of hot wax. I sat at my desk in the teetering light and tried to read my English composition students' response to their first in-class writing assignment. I had asked them to write a one-paragraph response to the question: *What is love?* Not wanting to waste paper, groups of four students shared one 8 $^1/_2$ x 11 sheet, carefully tearing it into quarters. Most wrote only a sentence or two.

---

[1]Stephanie Marlis, excerpted from her poem,"Days," *Manoa* (Honolulu: University of Hawaii Press, Summer 1995, vol. 7, no.1), p. 197.

Due to the wind I couldn't keep all of the wrinkled scraps of love weighted down, the candle lit, or the rain out, so I moved to another room, choosing hot and windless over inconvenient but cool. But without the breeze to distract me, the incessant pounding of rain on metal was barely tolerable. I couldn't hear myself think. I couldn't hear anything. I was consumed by the barrage of sound which refused to diminish, and then, after nearly an hour, amazingly, got louder.

The students who lived with us seemed not to notice the torrent of rain, or at least not to mind. Mhae, though she surely couldn't hear herself, was playing her guitar and singing with Lita. I watched them for a moment but couldn't tell what song they were mouthing. Narissa was studying intensely with a trio of thick candles set up around her. She had positioned them so the flames danced wildly in the wind but somehow were never extinguished. The shifting light and sinister shadows didn't seem to affect her concentration. Eden was outside on the porch talking to her boyfriend under the overhang. Carol was reading Jane Smiley's *A Thousand Acres* with a dim flashlight. I dreamt of Iowa, the place I will always come from. My corn and cows and October frosts had been replaced by rice and water buffalo and typhoons. I felt like one of Smiley's characters. I too was going nuts.

"Love is like the mango—ripe, sweet, everywhere. Everyone eat the mango. Everyone love."

"Love is patient and gentle—like slow bubbling rice."

"Love is feeling I have with family that we both know."

"I love Yang, our carabao. We depend for each other."

"My mother nursing her bebe—up all night. Love is what that is."

The students' responses pulled me out of my frustration. I was intrigued by the variety. When I give the same assignment at home in the U.S., my students, who are more adept at English, write less concrete responses. Most are close to this: "Love is a strong emotional feeling or bond which a person has for another person or thing." The whole idea of this introductory exercise is to distinguish between writing that tells or explains and writing that shows or reveals, to move from vague, abstract concepts to concrete imagery. It was interesting how the Filipino students seemed to more readily give examples, to show love rather than attempt to explain it. I wondered if there were any cultural implications.

"Caring is love. How do we care. When they dynamite fish in my place they are not caring about the coral. Now there are no fish. No coral or shell. Now there is no love."

"My brothers and I work together. We love to work together. We love each other. We trust each other."

"Love is not always so easy. Sometime I am hard up for love. Two boys courting me. They play the guitar for me, but I don't think it is love."

"Love is banal."

Love is "banal"? This response, one of the shortest and least concrete, confused me. In part because I hadn't heard the word since we had arrived in the Philippines. Love is dull, common, ordinary, and mundane? I wondered if I was missing something. Could she mean that love doesn't need to be extravagant or overly complicated, that it's necessary and habitual? I didn't think so, at least from the little I knew about "love" in Philippine culture. "Banal" would seem to describe what love is not.

I asked Lita for help.

"'Banal' means 'sacred' or 'holy,'" she explained.

"It does? I've never heard that definition."

"That's because you don't speak Tagalog," she smiled.

I told her that there was also a word in English spelled "b-a-n-a-l." She had never heard of it.

Just then Lita hurried off toward the door. "You're not going out are you?" I asked. "No, no, someone is tapping at the gate." How in the heck did she hear that? How did she distinguish that faint metallic tapping from the roar of the storm?

It was a neighbor. I'd forgotten her name again. She wanted to borrow a candle. Lita had some extras and went to get them. The woman, who was sopping wet despite her best efforts with her umbrella, sat down near me in the flickering light and smiled. "Adu!" ("A lot!"), she said, referring to the rain, trying to be cordial. "Demasiado" ("Too much") I replied. She laughed. It didn't seem to bother her that we were yelling. "No, no," she shouted, "Mayat!" ("It's good!"). "What?" I asked, reverting to English. She looked confused. "What? What is good?" I asked again. "The rain. The rain is good," she said, now in English. She pointed to the metal roof. "Listen," she said. The rain was actually beginning to let up—a machine-gun instead of a jackhammer overhead. "The roof sings," she said smiling again. "Huh? It what?" I asked. "Listen," she said. "The rain makes the roof sing." She looked at me like we shared a secret. I desperately wished we did. I understood what the sentence meant, but not her deep, knowing gaze. I wondered if she knew that my affirmative nod was in ignorance.

Lita returned with the candles. The woman said "Agiamanak" ("Thanks") and headed back out into the downpour.

I kept listening. I waited for the watery rhythms and melodies to reveal themselves. But nothing came. That was all I needed. I had found a specific inanimate target for my general frustration: the rain on the roof. But then the neighbor lady came along and exonerated it. She claimed the rain made the roof sing! I wondered why she was so happy. I wondered what kind of song or what kind of voice she heard. I wondered why I couldn't hear it. I wondered if I would ever hear the intricacy of Philippine culture above the constant hum of my own.

The next afternoon the rain almost stopped, dwindling to a soft drum. But two days of downpour had deadened my hearing. The depth of the quiet was overwhelming. I found myself yelling, still competing with the imagined sound of rain on metal. Narissa laughed when I spoke too loudly, joking about my needing a hearing aid.

I pulled out another folder of student writing. Just to vary things, I had asked this class (more than half were religion majors) to respond to the question, "What is God?"

"God is not here. I not believe now because of suffering much."
"God is hope."
"God walks in muddy fields. He plants seedlings—new life."
"God is what always there is."
"God is rice. God is rain."

God is rain? Was somebody trying to tell me something? That night after supper the rain completely stopped. It was replaced by the frogs in the flooded banana grove near our house. They were not as loud as the rain, but close. I lay awake sweating and listening to the great burping swamp of noise, the slippery green, cold-blooded chorus, swelling then waning, swelling then waning, seemingly without reason.

I paid closer attention. After an hour of listening I began to notice that this was not one huge croaking wave of sound, but a sea of specific croaks with different rhythms, tones, tunes—perpetually interrupting each other. Yet despite the seeming entropy, it was clear they were all singing one song. There was a kind of unity in the cacophony, an odd, unexpected harmony, a collection of sounds that were at once chaotic and healing. Harmony—sounds that sound good together precisely because they're different. That night something changed. I was beginning to hear things.

The next morning the typhoon was still going strong. Classes were canceled. I slid the capiz shell windows closed and pulled out some more student writing.

"God is always, but not one thing."
"God the source of all things is. God the creator and redeemer."
"God is espiritu *[spirit]—everywhere. I never wonder no God is here."*
"God? Seguro adda. Diak ammo. *But I think yes."*

The last two responses confused me. In Ilokano *adda* means "is present," and *diak ammo* means "I don't know." Since there

are a lot of Spanish words in Ilokano, I assumed that *seguro*
meant the same thing it did in Spanish: "certain." But that
didn't make sense: "God is certainly here. I don't know." Then
I remembered that some of the Spanish words were spelled
the same but had taken on different meanings during the
colonization process as they were integrated into Ilokano.
Seguro in Ilokano means "maybe," not "certain" as it does in
Spanish. I wondered about the historical implications of that.

Did the early Filipinos respond "seguro," ("certainly")
in the unquestioning affirmative to their Spanish masters,
but actually mean or think "maybe" in their unwillingness
to yield or acquiesce, in their longing for other options? Now
the phrase made sense. "Maybe God is here. I don't know,
but I think yes."

The next sentence also confused me: " I never wonder no
God is here." More multi-lingual confusion. I marveled at
how my students balanced the regional language (Ilokano),
the national language (Filipino), the language of instruction
(English), and often a tribal language or two. But with my
limited Ilokano and nonexistent Filipino, I was often confused by the occasional language-hopping in their writing.
Here one word caused the problem—*no*. *No* means "if" in
Ilokano. Again I wondered about the colonization process,
about Spanish or American conquistadors saying "no" and
Ilokanos learning to hear an "if," to hear possibility in denial
or condemnation, to see a crack of light seeping beneath a
locked door. "I never wonder if God is here." I found myself
longing for this student's certainty. But I was thinking more
about belief in myself than in God. I wanted to believe that I
could acculturate in an isolated rice farming community in
the Philippines. And I wanted to believe that I should be
teaching English, "the language of the colonizer," or "the language of money," as one of my students once characterized
it while explaining why English should be relegated to a foreign language.

I put the papers down and listened to the rain, wanting
to hear an "if" beyond all of the "no's" I had accumulated

while trying to live in a radically different culture, while awkwardly groping toward integration and acceptance. I started thinking about the English and Filipino definitions of "banal." Somehow the bilingual irony seemed related to the "if" I was looking for. How does one learn to see and hear the *banal* (Filipino) in the "banal" (English)? How does one learn to find meaning and value in what at first appears to be meaningless?

My students and friends were trying to help me understand. In their immense patience, they were trying to teach me to live in the present tense, to pay compassionate attention to the world, to listen and see carefully enough to discern the possibility of the extraordinary in the seemingly ordinary, to hear the sacred music in the off-centered, wooden rumble of two wagon wheels, and a slow, cloppity oxen, pulling a rice farmer and his son back to their land, back to that raw green rectangle of life. They were teaching me that "love is like a mango," that "God is rain," that frogs can croak harmony, that a "maybe" can be better than a "yes," and that an "if" is not always so far from a "no." They were teaching me about the writing process but also about the difficult process of crossing cultures.

A few hours later the typhoon finally waned. The torrents of wind faded, and the driving sheets of rain eased to a steady downpour. People took the opportunity to get out of their homes. They emerged from behind bamboo gates to see how the typhoon had left their world. Dozens of mangoes, still too green to bruise, had prematurely blown to soft thuds in the leafy soil around their wooden houses. Children collected them in plastic buckets. Then they began to pick up the wet green tangle of bougainvillea vines and broken acacia limbs. Finally, they swept up the tattered banana leaves with short stiff brooms made from the ribs of a palm frond. The dust pan was a large cracker tin cut away on one end and wired to a pole.

A vendor walked by balancing a long pole on the back of his neck with two silver pails at either end. "Mami! Mami!"

he called, peddling noodles. As the streets began to drain, horse-drawn carriages gradually reappeared. They taxied people to the market or on some other long-delayed errand. A neighbor rolled up her pantlegs and stretched a rice sack over her head for protection as she waded across the still-flooded banana grove. Three green coconuts, a hubcap, and a freshly drowned rat floated by her on the way. She stepped over the open sewer and up onto the street on her way to the corner sari sari store for some eggs.

I kept listening. The rain became light and easy. It softly tapped gentle, corrugated rhythms. The tapping evolved into a pinging, and I began to detect tinny, dented melodies. They unrolled themselves like banana leaves in the sun, their immense hidden beauty slowly revealing itself without warning or effort. A little later Carol finished her book and asked me if I wanted to go to the market with her to get some milkfish for supper. I told her I needed to finish my papers. But instead I kept listening to the roof, searching for the quiet, elusive voice of the rain.

Among the Philippine Missionaries, the desire to save the heathen from perdition emerges most clearly in the letters of Herbert M. Damon, who lived in Laoag. He eventually "felt the load of the heathen" upon him and experienced an "intense burden for the lost." Damon's position as a school teacher limited his effectiveness as a missionary however.

Kenton Clymer (with quotes from Damon's August 8, 1908 letter)[1]

A White Christmas

The Ilocos region, where Laoag is located, usually cools down to the low eighties by late November. But our first year there, a heat wave settled in near the end of the month and didn't dissipate until after Christmas. A simultaneous national energy shortage resulted in daily twelve-hour "brown-outs." No electricity meant no fans or ice for relief. So at dusk, after a hot, sweaty day of teaching, I often would sit outside under the brilliant green, motionless

---

[1]Clymer, *Protestant Missionaries in the Philippines*, p. 14.

51

leaves of the mango and banana trees. I graded papers or read the daily newspaper. One day a story on the front page caught my eye.

It Snows in Manila Today

Snow falls in Manila today, at least at SM Megamall, where Manila's Snow Funtasy, the first of its kind in the country, is having its grand opening.

"Almost 2000 square meters of space at the Megamall in Mandauyong are covered with permasnow or artificial snow that will look, feel, and even taste like the real thing," said Herman A. Eden, the German engineer and inventor of the snow technology.

For an entrance fee of 50 pesos ($2.00 U.S.) per adults and 40 pesos per child, visitors can view winter scenes, experience snowfall and make snowballs. There is a snow garden complete with igloos and stuffed penguins, Santa's workshop, a log house, several snow blanketed bridges, and a snowy scene of New York City, with views of skyscrapers, street signs, and lamp posts. There is also an activity area where people can actually handle and play with snow.

Filipinos dreaming of a White Christmas will finally have a chance to experience Snow Funtasy at SM Megamall until the end of January. Snow Funtasy is a project of Windsor Entertainment Corporation and Corps International Limited, Hong Kong, and Permasnow Inc., Australia.

I had been to SM Megamall and two other malls during our orientation and language study in Manila. SM City, the mall nearest our apartment, was the most interesting and disturbing, because of its location near a large squatter community. Before arriving, as I peered through the front window of the *Monumento* bus, through the black clouds of diesel exhaust, I would see the mall slowly materialize from a hot, wavy mirage into an imposing palace of cool, white granite: an island of wealth surrounded by sprawling poverty, by packs of street children and dogs straying in the dust, scrounging for scraps of food and hope.

Like malls in the U.S., Philippine malls are timeless, Muzak-filled escapes from the real world. Cool, controlled environments tailored to rapidly quench bodily and material thirsts without distraction. They are three times as crowded as U.S. malls. This may be because nearly two-thirds of all Filipinos live below the poverty line. There is more physical hardship, but fewer places to escape the grind of daily life—fewer public oases.[2]

The best part is that it's free. A free escape and free entertainment. Any who the armed entrance guards consider appropriately dressed can enjoy the air conditioning, ride the glass elevators, smell the bread in the French bakery, wander through rows and rows of imported underwear and polo shirts, and stay as long as they like. Those with money can try a Dunkin' Donut, an A & W Root Beer float, a Dairy Queen Blizzard, a Whopper, a Big Mac, a Wendy single, a Pizza Hut pizza, or a Kentucky Fried Chicken. They can in effect visit the U.S. without a visa or plane ticket. Since nearly 10 percent of the Filipino population (over six million people) currently have applications filed for a U.S. visa, but very few receive them, this is an attractive alternative. Particularly now, with the added possibility of a snowball fight and a pretend tour of New York.

But the marketing of snow in the Philippines, this glorification of U.S. ("Western") culture, is symbolic of the Philippines' ongoing struggle to outlive its colonial history and construct its own cultural identity. The greatest beneficiaries of a white Christmas in the Philippines are not

---

[2] Malls in the Philippines are booming in popularity and sales. Manila's largest mall, Mega Mall, increased its profits by 40% last year to $58 million in net profits (little of which benefits the poor majority in the provinces). The mall phenomena has taken its toll on the tiny Mom and Pop *Sari Sari* stores. They have decreased from 750,000 in 1975 to around 100,000 today. See "Malled: Retailing in the Philippines," *The Economist* (May 18, 1996), pp. 69-70.

Filipinos, but the Australia- and Hong Kong-based multinational corporations who are selling "exotic" Western climatology and other products with enormous success. They are the ones who hope that Filipinos are "dreaming of a white Christmas."

Another story in the same paper included a photo of Philippine President Ramos at Ninoy Aquino International Airport. He was part of a media event welcoming home hundreds of overseas contract workers for their vacations. Since one in twelve employable Filipinos works overseas, there were a lot of returnees. They came from Saudi Arabia, the U.S., Hong Kong, Italy, Kuwait, Japan, and Singapore, most toting suitcases and boxes full of treasures from the One-Third World. Ramos called the workers "a new kind of hero" for bringing foreign capital home to a desperate economy.[3] Ramos continues to believe that the Philippines' economic problems can best be solved outside the Philippines, by massive foreign investment, and by continuing to promote human beings as the leading Philippine export commodity. This "solution," however, has led to many related problems: a rapidly growing mail-order bride industry (each year approximately 19,000 Filipinas leave the Philippines to join husbands of different nationalities—mostly in the U.S.); a growing sex industry (many displaced Filipina workers overseas quickly slide into the "entertainment" professions—75,000 work in the Japanese sex industry alone); growing abuse problems among Filipina domestic workers abroad (many survive physical and/or sexual abuse and slave labor conditions in order to earn foreign currency).[4] And there is a more central social problem caused by overseas contract labor—the

---

[3]The Philippines is the world's largest exporter of human labor, and the remittance from that labor is the nation's largest source of foreign capital. In 1994, approximately five million Filipinos worked abroad, remitting approximately six billion dollars. See Jonathan Carp, "A New Kind of Hero," *Far Eastern Economic Review* (March 30, 1995), p. 43.

[4]Ninotchka Rosca, "The Philippines' Shameful Export," *The Nation* (April 17, 1995), p. 524.

ongoing disintegration of the extended Philippine family. Given the centrality of the extended family in Philippine culture, the impact cannot be underestimated.

The Ramos story reminded me of a "hero's" wife and daughter we had visited the previous week. Several years ago, Flor's husband, Jun, left to work as a driver in Riyadh, Saudi Arabia. This was one month after their daughter, Nieves, was born. Now he comes home every two years for one month. On their living room card table is a framed picture of the family. The picture of Jun was taken in 1991. The picture of Flor and Nieves was taken in 1993. She carefully snipped around the new picture of herself and her daughter and spliced it with the old picture of Jun so it seems they are still together, still in the same place. She does this several times a year. They are changing, though. Flor is heavier and wears her hair shorter. Nieves is getting taller and now plays the piano. But Jun always looks the same as the day he left for Saudi.

+ + +

A week after I read that it was "snowing" in Manila, some friends visited from Singapore. We took them to a nearby beach resort. It was the day after Christmas. We soon discovered that the village, Bauang, and the lodge where we were staying were completely supported by sex tourism, which booms over the Christmas holiday. Our lodge was run by an Australian and his American partner. Most of the guests were Americans, Australians, and Germans.

For two days I watched fat, middle-aged white men waddle in the sand like sunburnt penguins with small, young, brown women hanging on them. The men would tell stories in English and laugh. The women, who spoke little English, nodded and smiled a lot.

I talked to one of the men—Johnny, an American businessman. He had come to the Philippines for his Christmas vacation to escape the bitter Detroit winter. He explained his holiday sex tour package: a "white Christmas" in the Philippines.

"We pay the girls' managers 300 pesos [approximately $12 U.S.] per day plus drinks. They do pretty much anything we want. But most of the guys are nice to them. So it's good for them and it's good for us. They can't make this much fishing. (Laughing) Hell, it's good for the economy. 'Local sustainable development, ' they call it. And we feel good because not only are we helping the less fortunate, but we're rechanneling foreign capital. Everybody wins."

Our friends left for Manila the next day to catch their flight home. We returned to Laoag. We were having some guests over on New Year's Day and needed to prepare.

I got up early on New Year's and went outside to break off some *marunggay* leaves to season a big pot of *mongo* beans which I had put out to soak. As I tramped around in the thicket behind our house at 6:00 a.m., I realized why Christmas had seemed so strange this year. It wasn't the absence of snow or pine clippings or eggnog. I had accepted that. It was more that I had finally adjusted to the rainy season, to rain as a rhythm for daily life, and now it had stopped—completely stopped. I couldn't get used to the dry season, to the humidity settling in at sunrise, to occasional mangoes rather than rain booming on our metal roof, to the rice fields all being replanted with garlic, to what seemed like more umbrellas in the market than in the rainy season (protection for the vendors), to the raw blue, completely empty sky, and to a reliable yet relentless sun.

I went into the kitchen to reheat some fried bananas for breakfast when Bing Crosby eased on the local (normally non-English) radio station as smoothly as a bamboo *banca* onto the South China Sea at dawn. His croon slowly rose above the sizzling bananas and the hog grunts next door. The irony of the song in that context made me want to both laugh and cry. I wondered if I belonged in Laoag anymore than Bing did.

A few minutes later I heard our neighbor, singing outside. He was listening to the same radio station that I was but mocking the low swinging tones of Crosby's voice. He knew most of the words to the verses but had changed the chorus. "I'm dreeeaming of a browown Christmas," he sang, laughing as he built a fire to prepare breakfast.

+ + +

The college term began in mid-January. I was asked to teach a course in American literature as part of my first se- mester load, since it was part of the curriculum for English majors. But when I discovered that my students had read very little (if any) modern Filipino literature, I changed the course to comparative literature, contrasting several recent Filipino and American authors. I hoped that this would en- able us to explore the complex colonial tangles of Philippine and American identities, to consider why the students had so little accessibility to writers from their own country, to their own literary identity.

I went to the college library to get a feel for Philippine literature in English and other languages. Faculty and friends touted our library as the "biggest and best" in town, eclips- ing the other two local colleges and the university branch campus. I soon discovered that this was largely due to the thousands of donated books from various mission boards and international relief agencies.

The newest addition to the library was a "Filipiniana" cabinet—literature about Philippine culture and society. This small cabinet was locked. I got the key from the librarian and found ten novels and four anthologies by Filipino writ- ers. But that was it for modern Philippine literature.

I perused the main stacks looking for more. Eight shelves, or about one-eighth of the entire literature section, consisted of *The Reader's Digest Condensed Books* (from 1951-1983). I ran- domly pulled a few other books: *The Wit and Wisdom of Abraham Lincoln, The World's Best Fifty Speeches, The World's Best Short Stories, Emerson's Essays, Victorian Prose Masters,*

The Red Badge of Courage, and *Making It in the U.S.: A Handbook for Filipinos* (which was misshelved). Most of the "world's best" speeches and short stories were from the U.S. or England. None were from Asia. The first anthology I pulled was *Your World in Prose and Verse* (1960), which included Dickinson, Twain, Browning, Keats, Longfellow, Whitman, and others, primarily American and English classics. Inside the cover, a full-page color illustration featured two blond-haired, blue-eyed teenagers downhill skiing in beautiful snow-capped mountains. That day it was a hundred and five degrees, and there was still no electricity. Instructors had to yell to make themselves heard over the nearby shopowners' generators.

The lack of availability of Philippine literature was disheartening. But so was my students' "Dallas" and "Wheel of Fortune" perception of the U.S. (this was more common in the provinces than in Manila). A former student who had come to visit us over the holidays saw a picture of Suzanne Sommers on the cover of a *People* magazine and immediately turned to her friend and whispered something. After their short private discussion, they called me over, pointed out her light hair and skin, and then asked if she was a "pure American."

My students were both perplexed and curious about some of the American authors I had them read: Ralph Ellison, Maya Angelou, Rigoberta Menchu, and Pablo Neruda. These were "Americans" too? Americans are poor? They struggle for land and justice? Americans aren't white? The students resonated most with the stories and poems from Central America, given the similarity to their own culture.

One day I passed around a stack of five-by-seven black and white photos from some unnamed country. I asked the class to tell me what they could about the culture framed by the photo solely from close analysis. Finally, I asked them to guess where the photo was taken. All of the students guessed that all of the photos were taken in the Philippines. But I had actually taken them in Nicaragua. I wasn't trying to trick them but to clearly demonstrate the parallels between the two cultures, the similarity in conquests, climates, and cuisines. This led to an interesting discussion about conquest and culture formation.

I photocopied stories by the American authors and by various Filipino writers, and I put twentieth-century American and Filipino literature anthologies on reserve in the library. (Both were edited and published by Filipinos in the Philippines.) Ironically, the first poem that appeared in the American anthology was "Stopping by Woods on a Snowy Evening," by Robert Frost.

We discussed the cultural (ir)relevance of the poem, as well as its literary merits. I first asked if and how students identified with the poem. One student, whose family farmed rice, identified with the horse (though they didn't use or own one), the "woods," and the general rural feel. Another student said she didn't identify much with the poem, particularly with watching the "woods fill up with snow."

Hoping to spark discussion, I then asked how they would feel if U.S. literature were all they could read or study, or if Frost's poem instead appeared in the Philippine anthology. They thought this amusing, even ludicrous, until one student pointed out what many others knew: 90 percent of the literature in the college library is still from the U.S.! My students also knew that the primary reason we were reading modern Filipino writers was because I could afford to buy the new books in Manila and to photocopy sections for them.

After analyzing some of the literary merits of Frost's poem, we discussed the first short story in the Philippine anthology, "Harvest," by Loreto Para Sulit. The story is about the difficult relationship between two brothers who work together in the rice fields of Northern Luzon. The selfish older brother Fabian wants his younger brother Vidal to marry a woman he doesn't love in order to gain the five water buffalo which her family has promised if they marry. Though the diction and many of the metaphorical allusions in this story were more difficult than in Frost's poem, even the poorest English readers seemed to understand the plot, and everyone had stronger reactions to it. They understood the complexity of sibling relationships in the extended family, but more importantly, they understood the life of the rice farmer. As we discussed the plot and the characters, it soon became apparent how little I knew about rice farming, and about Philippine culture in general. I ended up mostly listening. The students discussed their interpretations of the two brothers' motives and the apparent themes the author was trying to draw out. In their excitement they began to shift from English (the language of instruction) to Ilokano (their first language—which I could follow somewhat), and to Filipino (the national language). Other times some shifted to Igorot, the regional language of the characters in the story. I couldn't follow that discussion, nor did I attempt to direct it back to English. Remi, a student sitting nearby, would occasionally translate for me. The class taught *me* the story, their story.

After we finished discussing "Harvest," I clumsily tried to connect the two disparate rural contexts (Frost's New England and Sulit's Northern Luzon) to our earlier discussion about the conflict between language and colonial culture. I asked the students to write down all the words they knew related to snow or winter weather in the U.S. Though at first puzzled, they wrote "snow," "cold," "ice," "cool," and "frozen." I added "frost," "sleet," "icicle," "glazed," "flurry," "blizzard," "slush," "blanket," "frigid" "bitter," "nippy," "bleak," and "wintry" to their list.

Then I wrote the word "rice" on the board. Though rice and rice farming is the heart of Ilokano culture, there was/is only one English word to describe it, to hold its meaning— "rice." I then asked the students to give me some words for rice in Ilokano. They came up with ten or twelve. These are the ones I remember: *banubon* (sprouts from seed), *raep* (the bunches of replanted seedlings), *palay* (rice in the field ready to cut), *irik* (separated grains but with husks), *bagas* (shelled and polished grains), and *innapoy* (cooked).

Given the implications of our exercise, we then discussed what it means for the once colonized to grow up studying the colonizer's culture. What does it mean to grow up idealizing hamburgers and snow instead of rice and rain? What does it mean for a Filipino to be an English major? (English remains the language of instruction at most colleges and universities in the Philippines.) How can one learn the meaning of Philippine culture in a language that can't hold it?

Pablito and Claire, articulate honors students majoring in history and English, seemed troubled by my questions about language and culture. Though they didn't say anything in class, later, after some prying and teasing, they asked me some hard questions. Their tone was more curious than confrontational, but I didn't hear it that way.

But with all respect sir, are you not from the U.S.? What does it mean that you are still teaching English grammar and U.S. literature in the Philippines? Are you also a part of the colonizing tradition?

Pablito's and Claire's honesty rekindled the colonial guilt and initial confusion I had felt when we first received a letter of invitation to teach in the Philippines. I had worried that my teaching position might in some way contribute to the ongoing conquest of "the developing world," a less obvious and perhaps more sinister mode of cultural imperialism. I wondered if I was really that different from the hundreds of English teachers who arrived on the *St. Thomas* in Manila Bay nearly a century ago intending to "civilize" the inhabitants of our new colony with raw ambition and boxes of English primers.

I was and I wasn't. I *was* still part of the problem. When a friend wrote asking if I didn't "feel a little funny about teaching English in a former colony," I got defensive. Yes, I was teaching English, the language of the colonizer, but it was also the language of instruction as decreed by the national government. Yes, I was teaching American literature, but it was only one of five courses, and it had been sanctioned by the Philippine Department of Education and the English department in the college. I just taught what they told me to teach. At a faculty meeting our college president had once pleaded with the faculty to speak only English. Several faculty questioned the long-term benefits of this approach. Wouldn't this work to the detriment of the national and regional languages (i.e., Filipino and Ilokano)? What would happen to their culture? The president, a wealthy man who had studied at Stanford for several years, worked himself into a frenzy. "It is for the students' own good!" he said finally. "If they want to succeed, if they want to get a good job, they need English!"

For better or worse, nearly a century of imposed American culture has infused Philippine culture, and now the two permanently simmer in a strangely tragic stew. The "ingredients" range from powerful multi-national corporations, like Dole and Del Monte, to a variety of indigenous tribes, like the Igorots and Aetas, who faithfully tend two-thousand-year-old rice terraces and still hold to the laws of ancestral domain. Madonna and McDonald's are certainly as popular in Manila as Sharon Cuneta and Jollibee's, their Philippine counterparts, but the interesting thing is that they're not much different. It is still much easier to find a Coke or Pepsi than a *buko* juice (coconut milk) on the streets of Manila, or even in the provinces. I met a number of people who called all toothpaste "Colgate," no matter what brand. My first day in Laoag I noticed a homemade bamboo and plywood basketball hoop across the street with "Chicago Bulls!" and "Go Michael!" painted on the backboard.

It is simplistic at best to pretend that American culture and the English language could somehow be eradicated from the Philippines, or that most Filipinos would want that. But at the same time I often felt caught between cultures, caught between the country I had come from and the one I lived in, caught between those who exonerated American culture and the English language, and those who remained critical and untrusting of their former colonizer. Pablito's and Claire's questions haunted me: Was I identifying and struggling with the Filipino people toward a self-determined cultural identity, toward socioeconomic autonomy? Or was I some well-meaning, multicultural romantic, who was unknowingly helping to maintain the neocolonial chains which still restrain many Filipinos?

Nearly a year after our return to Chicago, on a bitterly cold winter morning, I remember trying to crowd these questions out of my mind. Outside I watched the heavy, dark crook of an oak tree fill up with snow. I was reviewing multicultural freshman English anthologies for my spring classes. I had perused nine or ten but couldn't find one that suited me. Most were "American," some "global" or "international." The titles were all similar: *Global Voices, Diverse Identities, Crossing Cultures, One World, Many Cutures*, and so forth. It was a difficult choice. They all looked the same. Cultural diversity had become generic: a neatly packaged, highly marketable product.

On that snowy January morning, I realized that I hadn't encountered a single Philippine or Philippine-American writer in any of the texts. No Jessica Haggedorn, no Carlos Buloson, no Bienvenido Santos, no N. V. M. Gonzalez, no Ninotchka Rosca, no F. Sionil Jose, no Eric Gamalinda. Nobody.

It was within this enormous silence that I heard Pablito's and Claire's gentle, persistent voices. Their painful questions again rose to haunt me. In the years since our return to the U.S. I have found some comfort in a Filipino study group and in some Philippine writers, but no answers. The questions remain. They are heavy. They are teaching me.

Waiting for the Kin-dom

How long before the night gives way to the new dawn—so eagerly awaited but which seems to take forever to break out on the horizon?

Karl Gaspar,[1] writing from prison

W e spent the first two months of our assignment in Manila, an intensely polluted and congested city. The World Health Organization had just released a study of the world's mega-cities with the worst air pollution. Manila came out on top. The horrendous traffic jams contributed to this problem. I sometimes longed for the relative bliss of Chicago at rush hour.

It seemed we spent much of our time in Manila waiting. Waiting for the electricity to come back on (it was off daily from noon until 6:00 p.m.), waiting to cross a street (no elec-

---

[1]Karl Gaspar, *How Long?: Prison Reflections from the Philippines*, eds. Helen Graham and Breda Noonan (Maryknoll, N.Y.: Orbis Books, 1986), p. 76.

tricity, no traffic lights), waiting for the garbage collectors to come (dozens of bulging plastic bags of garbage that had been hung from trees or had been opened by dogs onto the street), waiting for the streets to drain (the water was often waist-high after a rain), waiting for someone to come and install a phone (no one ever did), and waiting fervently for tap water. There was very little. We caught what we could from the spigot in two thirty-gallon plastic trash cans. From this the five of us had to bathe, flush the toilet, and save enough to boil for drinking. Boiling had become more common even for locals since the water, like most other "necessities" in Manila, was becoming less and less reliable. In the evenings, usually around 7:00 p.m., we would hear a hollow but steady dribble hitting the bottom of the plastic container far below.

I share this focused description of our daily life not to highlight hardship but, to the contrary, to exemplify a middle-class existence in Manila. If the unpredictable infrastructure affected our lives so dramatically, one can begin to imagine how it affected *most* Filipinos, who had even less reliable access to water, electricity, sewers, toilets, and other necessities.

They also wait, but with much greater immediacy. For the 60 percent of Filipinos who find themselves below the poverty line, the waiting is a question of daily survival, not convenience. The statistics are sobering. One-quarter of Manila's twelve million residents are landless squatters. Nearly 100,000 street children comb Manila's traffic-jammed intersections in search of coins and crumbs. More than half of Filipino college graduates are unable to find work. Of the twenty-three million employable Filipinos, more than half are unemployed, underemployed, or have been forced to work outside the country. Human labor is the leading Philippine export. The Ramos Administration continues to surrender 40 percent of the national budget to the World Bank, the IMF, and other lenders, to pay off a still-escalating foreign debt. The resulting mad scramble for quick (short-term) solutions, for foreign currency and investment, has contributed to the alarmingly rapid destruction of the environment and once-plentiful natural resources. The aftereffects of the Mount Pinatubo and Mount Mayon eruptions, and other natural disasters, also continue to take their toll (1.5 million people have been displaced due to Pinatubo lahar flow since 1993).

How do Filipinos respond to this socioeconomic nightmare? They struggle to survive, and they wait. Flexibility is a Filipino trait that has been both lauded and criticized by the international media. On the positive side, Filipinos have been likened to their native bamboo, possessing the immense flexibility and resilience necessary to endure four centuries of brutal colonialism. On the negative end, they have been criticized for their inability to achieve a revolution that will lead them out of their historic victimization and colonial dependency, that will radically change rather than mildly reform existing unjust social and economic structures. One might say that they have been admired for their tenacious ability to survive but criticized for waiting too long.

Waiting. How long? For whom? These are the questions that hung in the hot, dirty Manila air, as I exited our apartment each day onto Epifanio de los Santos Avenue (EDSA)— the same street that was flooded by thousands of joyous Filipinos at the climax of the 1986 people power movement a decade ago. But though this movement led to short-term political empowerment (i.e., the ouster of U.S.-backed dictator Ferdinand Marcos), it did not lead to economic empowerment. Six years of Corazon Aquino left the massive poor majority in a worse socioeconomic state that when they flooded EDSA. The Ramos years have not offered significant improvement. There are more malls and fewer brownouts. Filipinos still struggle to survive, and they wait. But many dare to hope.

Surviving, waiting, and daring to hope are central to the "Theology of Struggle." This Filipino brand of the liberation theologies I experienced in Central America developed similarly but is also as unique as the context which continues to define it.[2] Many Filipino theologians have commented that the theology of struggle is only beginning to be documented, because those who might do the writing are too involved in the struggle to have time. The struggle itself is all-consuming. Given the necessity of active participation, it is perhaps best defined as a theo-praxis of struggle. The unwritten "texts" for this theo-praxis come from the concrete experiences that rise from the struggling communities, from their stories. These narratives have been created and shared in a variety of forms: paintings, murals, and other visual arts, poetry, street drama, and music. It is both the grass-rootedness and in-process nature of the Theology of Struggle that encourages this kind of creative contribution. I utilize this methodology in sharing the following story of struggle, a narrative poem I wrote after a visit to Tondo, a large poor barrio in Manila.

Where Power Comes From

Eighteen families spliced electric lines to one pole
outside Rosa's second story window.
Through that suspended bramble of stolen power,
that buzzing tangle of hope(lessness),
she watches the rain,
her street become a river.

She turns on a light. Plugs in an iron.
Bolts of energy, dreams,
surge through the cracking maze of cables,
the snarled lives—desperate
to escape.
No exit.

---

[2] The most recent and comprehensive text on the theology of struggle is Eleazar Fernanado's *Toward a Theology of Struggle* (Maryknoll, N.Y.: Orbis Books, 1994).

Brownout.
Eighteen tin and plywood compartments go black.
Dozens of brains clench, curse the dark heat.
Mothers pick up crying babies, lean out window frames,
wait for a breeze,
or the sound of laughter.

Someone out on the pole in the rain
mends hot, jumbled wires
with soft, open hands.
The power returns.

Nine radios overwhelm a frantic child's scream,
a tinny, five string guitar,
a pan of hiss-popping empanadas,
and a bolo whack-whacking a coconut husk.
Rusty fan blades labor to a whir,
move heavy air and frustration to new locations.
Naked bulbs in muddy kitchens
startle the rats, scatter cockroaches,
elongate days so that they don't end.

Stolen power is unreliable.
Last month Fely died playing in the flood waters.
A wire snapped, sizzle-danced on his head,
short circuited his heart.
He washed down the street like a dead fish.

When Rosa remembers her son,
that wild blur of rain, the drifting corpse,
the bobbing coconuts, the pair of swirling sandals,
and his dog,
madly thrashing in the torrent
toward anything and nothing,
she wonders where power comes from—
who will lose the next Fely
for a radio or fan.

The lives of Rosa and Fely are theological texts that reveal the complexity, suffering, and resistance in the Filipino struggle for life. Poems, plays, songs, and other art forms can document the stories of struggle in evocative imagery that catalyzes theological reflection for a wide audience. Rosa's struggle for both electrical and spiritual power, and her lament over her son's drowning, will precede and shape the theologizing, the God talk. Her experience may initiate both social analysis and theological reflection: What are the reasons for the energy shortage? Why must Filipinos steal power? What kinds of power are needed in poor communities? Why does God not *empower* Filipinos? Why must they take such dire risks to survive? Is surviving enough?

Other stories I gathered over eighteen months suggested to me that the Philippine struggle exists on at least two levels: the immediate struggle for daily survival, and the longer-term struggle to construct what is best described by Cuban theologian Ada Maria Isasi-Diaz's term, "the *Kindom* of God." Simply put, to construct the Kindom of God is to build a society which is based on the physical and spiritual sustenance of the majority rather than on the satiation of the few (as exemplified by the Marcos "kingdom"). It is the construction of a socioeconomically just society where all are valued, and come to see each other as necessarily related, as *kin*. Given the centrality of the extended family, one would think that this concept would be particularly appropriate in the Philippines.

But on a visit to a poor Manila *barangay* (neighborhood), I discovered that it wasn't so simple. We spent the night with a U.C.C.P. pastor and his family. We sat on the wooden floor eating rice and fish, drinking Coke, and talking.

Pastor Lumabao, a long-time practitioner of the Theology of Struggle, explained its uniqueness.

The theology of struggle differs from Latin American and other liberation theologies. Part of our ongoing "struggle" is to define and construct a Philippine identity. Who exactly are "the people"? There are over 7000 islands and nearly eighty languages. We struggle to overcome our geographic division and cultural diversity.

I think many Latin American countries have a much clearer sense of national identity.

As I listened, I began to understand the difficulty of building national unity, of constructing the Kindom in the Philippines. It also became more clear why the Spanish, the U.S., and the Japanese had been such successful exploiters. The dividing part of the "conquer and divide" strategy had already been done for them.

Pastor Lumabao continued.

The theology of struggle also differs from some of those other liberation theologies in that we cannot focus primarily on the "liberation." Sometimes I think that we are still struggling toward the desert, that we remain in a state of bondage. Look around you. What do you see? The struggle, the suffering—it's everywhere.

Given the country's immense cultural diversity (potential for disunity) and dire socioeconomic state, I asked how he maintained hope or even imagined a Kindom. How did he prevent the theology of struggle from evolving into a theology of suffering? His answer was not complicated.

We believe in the living God, that wherever there are people struggling for justice there is hope. God is there. But suffering is also a part of it.

This response helped me better understand the theopraxis of struggle in the lives of many of the people we encountered in the Philippines. They often suffered, usually survived, and expected to wait. The thousands of unemployed prostitutes in Olongapo (the former site of Subic Naval Base) and their Amerasian children, the Irayan people struggling to protect their land against a Japanese mining corporation, the children and their parents who scavenged tin and paper on Smokey Mountain (which was later demolished because it was deemed bad international P.R.), the squatter community in Quezon City that has begun fighting for and securing housing leases from the government, the peasant farmers in Antipolo who literally lay down in front of the housing developers' bulldozers to prevent them from continuing to destroy their small farms and fruit trees, and the pastors and students in the college of ministry at our college who worked long hours at small isolated churches for a few hundred pesos ($30–50 U.S.) a month, or perhaps for no money at all, for a few chickens, some rice, and a place to sleep.

All of these people seemed to lead miraculous lives. Some simply because they were able to survive. Others because they were able both to survive and to hope, to attempt to co-create with God, to build something from almost nothing, to construct the Kindom from a life of struggle.

But lest I romanticize the Filipino struggle, it is essential to remember that building the Kindom is a difficult and painful process—in the Philippines, but also in the U.S. This is easy for affluent American Christians to forget. Probably because waiting, surviving, and physical suffering are as foreign to most of our daily lives as chicken *adobo* and the rainy season. Perhaps the question then is what can we in the One-Third World learn from the Filipinos' theo-praxis of struggle? How are we building the Kindom in our own context? What are *we* waiting for?

*Christ must be
a Filipino if Filipinos
are to be Christians.*

Edicio de la Torre[1]

Christ in a Philippine Context

Written with
Luna Dingayan[2]

Besides listening for and gathering the stories of the people in our community, we also attempted to collect Filipino interpretations of the Christian story—their understanding of the Bible and of Jesus given their unique context and history, given four centuries of colonization and struggle. After several conversations, Luna Dingayan, a pastor and theologian, and I co-wrote the following essay. It is an attempt to better understand the evolving meaning and perceptions of Christ in the Philippine context.

Here the difficulty of "implementing" the theology of struggle that Pastor Lumabao described in the preceding

---

[1]Edicio de la Torre, *Touching Ground, Taking Root: Theological Reflection and Political Reflection on the Philippine Struggle* (Quezon City, Philippines: Socio-Pastoral Institute, 1986).

[2]Luna Dingayan teaches theology at Ecumenical Theological Seminary in Baguio, Philippines.

essay is critiqued in light of the history of Philippine Christology. It is interesting that despite the enormous differences between our cultures, progressive Protestant Philippine churches (i.e., the United Church of Christ in the Philippines) face many of the same challenges similar churches do in this country. Conservative, fundamentalist churches that provide ready-made theologies with immediate "answers" are also growing rapidly in the U.S. (and Latin America).

The most popular understandings of Christ in the Philippines do not focus on Jesus' radical calls for a socio-political transformation of society. They do not focus on the political Jesus who preached liberation for the suffering peasant majority. They speak instead of a personal Jesus, a healer and miracle worker.

Since this view of Christ is increasing in popularity in so many other countries (including the U.S.), it seems worth considering its evolution in the Philippines. Perhaps in so doing we will better understand how progressive Christians and liberation-minded theologians need to modify or enhance our message.

As in so much of the world, massive economic injustice rages at every level of Philippine society. Yet the churches that are thriving in the Philippines do not demand that *dagiti tattao* (the people/believers) make an effort to confront that injustice. Rather, they welcome believers into a comforting spiritual community, where they are recognized as suffering individuals who need support on a personal level. The theology stressed in such churches offers eternal life in the next world and multiple forms of relief in this one.

Given the necessarily "day-by-day" lifestyle of many Filipinos, it's not difficult to understand why such churches are successful. Rather than focusing on economics and political structures in the future tense, these churches focus on pressing issues created by present social structures. They concentrate on how individuals can survive the struggles of today.

These striving churches recognize that Filipinos both inside and outside the remnants of the "people power" revolution are tired of failed political structures, empty jargon, and corrupt, immoral leadership. They realize that most people seek a faith and a Christ that provide clear-cut answers, not questions. They seek a faith that will give structure to unstructured lives. The Philippines, like so many countries, is filled with believers who seek some relief and hope *now*, not at the end of some complex social shift and far-off economic redistribution plan.

Two competing understandings of Christ, similar though different, have captured the hearts of most Filipinos. An analysis of those views can be instructive for all of us who care deeply about connecting Christian spirituality to issues of social and economic justice.

Perhaps the most popular image of Christ in the Philippines is that of the Holy Child, referred to as the *Santo Niño*. This image, frequently reproduced in visual art and statuary, depicts Christ as a beautiful, innocent child adorned in royal, kingly garb.

Earnest devotion to the Santo Niño is a distinctive mark of Roman Catholicism in the Philippines. People from all walks of life are remarkably devoted to this image. From squatters' huts to elegant chambers in Malacañang Palace, the Santo Niño is displayed. You'll find it in sari sari stores and big shopping malls. You'll see it in private and public offices, cars, jeepneys, buses, and even some nightspots.

The Santo Niño image was brought to the Philippines by the Spanish in the seventeenth century. But devotion to it was practiced only in Cebu (a southern island) until the Marcos years, when the first family's fervent devotion to the Santo Niño spread throughout the nation. Imelda Marcos, for example, was said to have had a Santo Niño image in nearly every room in Malacañang Palace, including her private bathroom.

There are several reasons for Filipinos' devotion to the Santo Niño. Many view it as a talisman or charm which will bring them good luck—or protect them from disasters like flood, fire, hunger, or disease. Students taking exams, business people, political candidates, and individuals afflicted with illnesses from headaches to cancer all appeal to the Santo Niño for help. Typically, the petitioners promise the Santo Niño that if their appeals are granted, they will give him gifts and more devotion.

Unfortunately, the Santo Niño models some of the more destructive life patterns of Filipinos—innocent, vulnerable, compliant, completely dependent. The Santo Niño also emulates the relationship between indigenous Filipinos and the "mother" church (Rome) and the "mother" country (first Spain, then the U.S.).

Critics of the Catholic hierarchy argue that the Catholic Church has maintained the Santo Niño imagery because it doesn't want the baby Jesus to grow up. They say the Catholic hierarchy finds an adult Jesus too dangerous, for he might be perceived as a revolutionary who sides with the marginalized (that is, with average Filipinos), preaching social justice.

Another popular understanding of Christ in the Philippines has evolved specifically from the Protestant evangelical tradition. It seems to have been initiated by a swell of electronic and parachurch organizations and charismatic groups during the Marcos era. Historically, Protestant fundamentalism has been present in the Philippines since the coming of American missionaries. But the social climate of martial law through the seventies simultaneously silenced the radical sectors in society and catalyzed the rapid growth of theologically conservative churches.

In recent years, tract distribution, street evangelism, and the electronic church have been booming in the Philippines. Fundamentalist churches of various kinds have captured the mass media—television, radio, newspapers—in ways that mainline Protestants were never able to do. This has facilitated the rapid dissemination of a conservative theology, simultaneously causing division and confusion in many mainline Protestant churches.

Spurred by Campus Crusade for Christ's "Four Spiritual Laws" and "I Found It" campaigns, along with Pat Robertson's Christian Broadcasting Network, conservative churches in the Philippines are continuing to grow.

These churches' understanding of Christ is central to their success. It is an understanding that has been adopted not only by many evangelical Protestant churches, but by some charismatic Roman Catholics as well. We might call it "passport theology," because Christ is viewed primarily as a passport to heaven. If you want to go to heaven, you must have a passport, meaning you must believe in Jesus Christ.

This dramatic oversimplification of the gospel message is typified by "Free Trip," a popular tract distributed by Overseas Missionary Fellowship. It is written in the form of a letter:

Dear Friend,

You are invited to travel with me free on a trip I will soon be making. This place is so beautiful I cannot describe it. The travel guidebook says even angels live there. But in order to go, you must have a special passport.

The place is heaven. The travel guidebook is the Bible (Revelation 21 and 22 in particular). The special passport is receiving Jesus Christ as your Savior.

If you have never been invited, I want to personally invite you to go to heaven with me. Just pray this little prayer with me if you want to go to heaven....

A clear example of this passport theology occurred recently in Manila. After an extensive six-month promotional campaign, including thousands of posters and radio spots, plus numerous "seminars" throughout the Philippines, the Mission for the Coming Days (based in Korea), called all of its followers to a large Manila church. Several hundred gathered in their white muslin robes on the afternoon of October 28 and waited. They believed the posters and tracts that read: *Rapture: October 28! Human history will end!*

About 2:00 a.m. on October 29, most of the believers went home disappointed. They squeezed into jeepneys and buses in their now sweaty, stained robes, and went back into the harsh reality of daily life in Manila. Their "passport" had not taken them to the golden throne in the sky. It had cost them a night's sleep and 150 pesos for a useless robe. They returned to their plywood and corrugated steel homes and made rice.

Both of these portrayals of Christ were originally propagated in the Philippines by non-Filipinos. They are theologies borrowed from foreign contexts, and their function has been to control and pacify rather than liberate the Filipino people. Both also oversimplify the human problem. This may be due in part to their origin in the One-Third World, a context that, relatively speaking, is not marked by a great deal of struggle.

The Santo Niño understanding of Christ reduces faith to an idolatrous obedience aimed at securing material rewards and avoiding material punishments. If the individual believer is not sufficiently devoted to the Holy Child, disasters and failure will dog his or her footsteps. If the individual believer is sufficiently devoted, he or she will be sufficiently rewarded. Human misery and suffering are interpreted primarily in this light.

In "passport" Christianity, the human problem is sin, interpreted primarily as the individual's separation from God. There is little or no mention of societal or institutional evil. To restore the broken relationship, the individual must repent and believe in Jesus, a step often accomplished by a prescribed prayer. When this relationship is properly reestablished, the believer is assured a passport to heaven.

Ironically, the popular appeal of these theologies may be precisely their theological weakness: they overtly avoid the real human problem of poverty. In focusing on material rewards and punishments (miracles and quick fixes) or on passports to the next world (individual rather than communal salvation), these understandings of Christ alienate the Filipino people from the realities of life in this world. They help to perpetuate a climate of passivity, fatalism, and superstition. They create a culture that cannot understand the essential theological relevance of its unique context—a context of poverty and struggle.

But there are no simple solutions to the Philippines' extensive socioeconomic problems. Nor is there an easy, painless understanding of Christ that will sustain people as they face the challenge of daily life. Nevertheless, some Christians in the Philippines believe and identify with a struggling Jesus. This understanding also offers hope in that it reminds Filipinos that their history has purpose and meaning, that despite what this nation has endured for five hundred years, there is more to life than exploitation, suffering, and death. It reminds them that they can work and struggle for a just, humane social order—because in the struggling, historical Jesus, such possibilities have been revealed.

Though this view is not yet popular, there have long been Christians in the Philippines who have sought to embody the relevance of this understanding. Day after day they seek to know the Christ who lived, worked, and struggled with a community of have-nots—with the unemployed, with squatters, with jeepney drivers, with candy vendors, with landless rice and fruit farmers, with fisherfolk, with prostituted women and children.

Icons and passports may seem to offer immediate "answers" or "relief" to Filipino Christians, but in the long run, such understandings cannot help but lead to a privatized theology that has limited connections to daily life.

Nevertheless, advocates of the theology of struggle need to learn something from these more popular understandings of Christ. Despite their flaws, there are elements we, too, need to hear. And perhaps it is time that we, with humility, begin to alter our approach.

It is becoming increasingly apparent that faith communities must not only understand the Christ of history but also find creative ways to spiritually nurture people in the present tense, during the course of the struggle. Rather than focusing only on political schemes for getting to the promised land, we need to focus on how to spiritually survive the daily bondage, the sojourn in the desert. We need new language, new liturgy, and new ritual to offer hope and strength *now*, not just in the future.

Second, we need to learn to keep at the forefront a Christ who is both personal and political. We need to realize that a personal relationship with Jesus Christ is not only valid and important—but can constitute a solid inspiration for political action.

Third, we need to break from the Spanish Catholic tradition and focus less on Christ's suffering and crucifixion as the only model for Christian living. The struggling Christ also overcame death, as "passport" Christians so effectively remind us. Through his resurrection, Jesus brought new hope and new life to his struggling community.

Additionally, we need to learn how to use the media. People all over *are* participating in theologies of liberation and struggle, in both rural and urban *barangays* (neighborhoods) throughout the Philippines. But you never hear about it in the mass media. Among those who follow the struggling Christ, few know what others within the community are doing. We need to improve our communication with each other and learn how to use radio and television to communicate our message to the masses. We also need to systematize our theological process so we can produce more accessible resources to share our ideas with a wider audience.

Most importantly, the theology of struggle must reinterpret the meaning of *conversion*. Conversion is a continuous process of renewal which requires both *repentance* and *commitment*. This means repenting for wrongs committed, both personal and social: for martial law and its legacy, for bulldozing squatters, for denuding forests, for dynamiting fish, and for ignoring and abusing tribal Filipinos and their families. We must repent for encouraging exploitive short-term "development" projects by multinational corporations, for exporting our best minds and bodies in the quest for foreign capital, and finally for the often conscienceless actions and policies of a powerful, elite minority in government, business, and the military. They continue to gamble away the lives of the powerless majority with their dollars and double standards.

At the same time, we must seek commitment to the possibilities of new life—to protecting our natural resources and environment, to mending our fragmented families broken by contract labor abroad, to encouraging local development projects, to recreating life and a sense of home for the millions displaced by Pinatubo lahar or other natural calamities, and to reestablishing a just social, political, and economic order in which all Filipinos are physically and spiritually sustained.

In short, Filipinos must recommit to believing in their own resurrection. And ironically, this may be the greatest struggle of all.

FILIPINO VOICES

III

In keeping with the central focus of this book, co-mission as a two-way process of cross-cultural education, the following essay by Leny Mendoza Strobel offers a Filipina's critique on much of what precedes. Her personal story, her analysis of mission and missionaries, of neo-colonization, and of evolving Filipino identities (both in the Philippines and in the U.S.), chronicles her own lifelong process of decolonization.

Undoing the Colonial Gaze

by Leny Mendoza Strobel[1]

E ver since Mount Pinatubo erupted, I have been trying mentally to paint a new landscape of my hometown in the Philippines. I remember a merry childhood, playing under moonlit nights and chasing each other's shadows. But *lahar*, flowing lava, reshapes the land and changes the people forever.

N. V. M. Gonzales, a Filipino-American writer, calls the Philippines "a *lahar* of colonizations." My own experience at regaining my identity confirms this. I have spent years learning to re-imagine my interior landscape because of this colonization.

In the 1950s, I lived in San Fernando, Pampanga—a town fifteen miles southwest from Mount Pinatubo, ten miles south

---

[1]Leny Mendoza Strobel currently teaches ethnic studies at Sonoma State University.

of Clark Air Base (then the largest U.S. military base in Asia), and fifty miles north of Manila. It was a growing rural town surrounded by farming and fishing barrios. We lived a mile away from the town plaza, built by Spaniards. The Catholic church, fronted by a big courtyard, faced the Municipio. Outside the courtyard, in the open market, the fishermen and farmers brought their fresh catch and produce and competed for the attention of women who carried a basket in one hand and a baby in the other. Across from the market, the grocery, shoe, and dry-goods stores owned by Chinese merchants served the needs of the local elite, who sought refuge from the melee outside.

By the time I was born, Methodists had built a small church near the town plaza. Unlike the Catholic church, it had no domes or turrets. It had a plain wooden cross (without the crucified Christ) atop the wooden scaffold beams, where bats made their home by day, retiring to the sanctuary by night. I grew up in this church.

I was raised with white, middle-class, Protestant values within an animist context by a Catholic mother and a Methodist father, both of whom had Chinese and Spanish ancestors. I didn't know it then, but we were poor. We had "class and good taste" and lived as genteel and "civilized" a lifestyle as possible—in keeping with what we were taught by our colonizers to be "genteel and civilized." Thus, we had Friday evening concerts with Bach and Mozart—my mother on the piano and my brother on the violin. My sisters and I sang in harmony with Cole Porter and Irving Berlin.

Before we had television, our radio was always tuned in to Frank Sinatra and Nat King Cole and sometimes to Voice of America. We read Hans Christian Andersen fairy tales, not Tagalog comics. We read English-language newspapers and magazines, not *Liway-way and Ibulaklak*, which were read only by the *bakya* crowd.

We lived this lifestyle in the midst of a neighborhood where the women sat on their front steps picking each other's lice while they exchanged the latest news and *tsismis*, where the men squatted on the sidewalk grooming their fighting roosters, drinking beer, smoking cigarettes, and telling ribald jokes punctuated by obscene words and gestures. Dogs, cats, and pigs roamed freely in this little hamlet, and the horses that pulled the *calesas* were fed in stalls built right outside the ten-foot-high cement walls of our backyard.

My world was also inhabited by spirits, superstitions, and omens. I heard ghost stories of visits from departed relatives and of spirits who possess those who offend the gods. And then there were superstitions. When the cat washed itself, we anticipated visitors. When our palms itched, we were told to anticipate money. When I swept the floors and moved the dirt toward the door, my mother scolded me for driving away good fortune.

My father drove the animist world underground. "As Protestants," my father said, "we do not believe in such things." Every night he led us in Bible readings and prayers. Yet every day my mother reminded us to be careful not to offend the spirits, not to cross their paths without asking permission. For she believed that the hills and the big *narra* trees were home to gnomes and dwarves. And that the *tikbalang* or the *aswang* would come and get little girls if they were not home by sundown. These other-worldly creatures played an active role in our fearful imaginations.

The end of May was fiesta time in our community, but not in my home. Evening processions of the *Santo Niño* and *Virgen de los Remedios*, murmured Hail Marys, and the pitter-patter of wooden *bakya* on the asphalt pavement met with awed silence. The light of flickering candles in the dark, veiled heads, and hands wrapped in rosary beads evoked feelings of awe and eeriness at the same time. But Protestants didn't believe in saints, much less in processions and chanted prayers; and so we watched "them" with the self-righteousness of Pharisees.

Fiesta brought wanted and unwanted guests to the neighborhood. But never to our home. Father forbade my mother to cook and forbade all of us from inviting relatives and friends. "Fiestas are for worshiping the saints," he said, "and we do not worship saints." So, for many years, May was the saddest time of the year.

Things changed the day my sister, who had been teaching Filipino culture at the dependents' school at Clark Air Base, asked to bring to the town fiesta a Yankee from Maine, the school's administrator. Perhaps it made my father glad that this very important White man was interested in my sister. Although he relented cautiously about breaking a family nontradition, he soon found himself making plans to roast one of the pigs he had been raising to supplement his income and pay our tuition. That year Junior the pig was sacrificed in honor of the White man.

I was assigned to make sure the house was clean, especially the toilet and the toilet bowl. When no amount of muriatic acid would erase the yellow-stained bowl, my sister handed me a copper penny and told me to use it to scrape the stain. For hours, I sweated on my knees, scraping the yellow.

This left a mark in my soul that I wouldn't understand for many, many years. I learned then that yellow isn't good enough. Only white will do.

White America maintained a strong presence in our lives. The shadow of Clark Air Base and the mystique of its isolation and separation by miles of barbed-wire fences and guarded military outposts awed us. In the 1960s, Peace Corps volunteers appeared in our schools. And my mother had a pen pal, Miss Rose B. Mann, from Pennsylvania. Every year we looked forward to our Christmas package of old Christmas cards, secondhand clothes, bags, and old magazines. Packages from the States smelled fresh, earthy, and musky. "The States smells good and clean," we told ourselves. "It must be heaven."

I made sure that I was liked by all the White missionaries and Peace Corps volunteers who came to visit us. I was fascinated by them. My young adult life became a series of attempts to approximate Whiteness in my tastes for American fashion, food, music, movies. I started calling my father and mother Dad and Mom instead of *Tatang* and *Ima*. My friends and I spoke English outside the classroom, even when it wasn't mandatory.

It became a full-time occupation for me to reach out to White folks, hoping for Whiteness to rub off, and to test myself by how well I could maintain their friendship and interest while waiting to hear some affirmation of our friendliness and the famous "Filipino hospitality." Sometimes we were rewarded by an invitation to their homes for dinner, to ride in their cars (always on the way to a religious meeting), and occasionally to the exclusive country club surrounded by high walls open only to White folks.

In my determination to win approval in their eyes, I wasn't conscious of the foreign words raining down upon us which devalued my culture and lifted up their own.

And so it came to pass. My American (mis)education became complete when I married a White man and came to the United States to live in the master's house.

What seemed at the time like a new beginning was actually the beginning of the end. My shattered expectations and the failure of religious structures and enculturated Christianity to explain them caused a deafening dissonance.

This dissonance was produced by White folks' looks and malicious questions: Are you married to a GI (read: are you a prostitute)? Are you a mail-order bride (read: are you for sale)? Do you know of a maid (read: are you a domestic worker)? When I was not taken for a Filipino, I was glad.

Nothing in my theology prepared me for God's silence to my many questions. If I'm a child of God, why do I feel intimidated by White people who are better-educated, talk faster, laugh louder? If I'm a child of God, how come White Christians do not treat me like one? Why don't they ask me intelligent questions? And why do they assume I'm a mail-order bride or married to a GI? If I'm a child of God, why am I not satisfied with spiritual answers to my questions?

There was no one to turn to. My sister (who married the other White man) said: "It will take time. Someday you will feel better."

If I had waited for that day, I would have ended up in a mental asylum. I became angry at what I didn't understand. I blamed myself, and I blamed God for betraying me.

How could God have brought me to this land only to shatter me and condemn me to live in confusion and utter despair amidst a sea of White people who are as cold and distant as the gaze in their eyes? These people whom I was taught to love, imitate, cherish, respect, envy—they all had betrayed me.

I sought out a famous Christian writer. By virtue of his having lived as a missionary to Africa, I hoped he would understand my confusion and answer my questions. He told me: "America is the greatest country in the world. Therefore, third-world people look up to the United States. We become a frame of reference for everybody." My tacit agreement with this conclusion drove me further into the abyss, and my feelings of inferiority and intimidation grew.

From then on, there was nothing but the pressure to assimilate—to act, talk, and walk like a White person. I wanted to belong, and I thought the only way to belong was to be like someone else. The resulting feelings of alienation were too heavy a price to pay. Finally, I stopped paying. I had to look elsewhere for answers.

A writer named Bhaba once commented, "Remembering is never a quiet act of introspection or retrospection. It is a painful re-membering, a putting together of the dismembered past to make sense of the trauma of the present."

Often during those painful days, thoughts of my grandmother visited me. Perhaps she was watching over me and wanted to remind me that I am loved. I remembered her stringing fragrant buds of *sampaguita*. Always gather the buds at dusk when their fragrance is not wasted in the heat of the sun, she admonished. While I helped her string, she would assemble her *mamman*—the betel nut, lye, a green leaf as wrapper—and put it in her mouth. Then she told stories.

I thought of my mother, a strong-willed woman with a quiet spirit. Her sense of self was unobtrusive, but she knew how to have her way when she wanted to. I thought of her as a piano teacher and music maker—that was her special space.

I rewrote their stories in my memory, seeing them in a new light. My mother, who in her boxed-in world, created a place where the ancient spirits never died. How did she resist the negation of her Catholic faith and her voice in a patriarchal home? How did my grandmother raise seven children alone when her young husband died?

I thought of my father. I wondered if he would ever find a place for himself outside the colonial gaze. Is there a space where he can be reconciled and at peace? When he had a chance to come to the master's house, he decided abruptly to go back home—did he, too, face the White master and shudder at what he had become?

Slowly it dawned on me that I was tapping into an inner resource through my memories. This unnamed source whispered to my tired soul, telling me that before there were Spaniards and Americans, there were peoples who sang, danced, lit the fire by night, and told each other stories about *Malakas at Maganda*, and about *Biag-ni-Lam-Ang*. There were women who healed, women who tilled the land alongside the men, and women who wove baskets and cast bronze into earrings, necklaces, armbands, and anklets.

But these were faint memories, buried underneath an avalanche of foreign words. There were no words for what I felt in my bones—not in English anyway. Was this possible—that before we were colonized and called lazy, backward, primitive, people in the dark, we already had known the wisdom of the ancients and lived under the guidance of our *anitos*? That we already knew who we were until we learned that we had better believe their definitions of us—or be killed?

"You are wild. You need to be Christianized. You must get rid of your superstitions. We will teach you how to become like us. We will unite your divided selves by giving you our language. We are your fathers, you are our children. By the grace of God, we will make you civilized yet."

And so we became like them. I did. I married my oppressor.

There is freedom in this confession. With it, I acknowledge that the self constructed by the colonizer was a false self. I came to see that the "damaged" culture described by the colonizers was nothing but a projection of their own failure at this grand imperial experiment. I understood then that when White people judge me harshly, it is because I remind them of their own shadow sides, their own failure to heal the split in themselves.

These discoveries gave rise to anger and defiance. How could I help it? I didn't know I had a voice; its timbre and resonance of truth were so long denied. Perhaps soon the anger will be spent, and I will be able to move on.

There is no place I can go to escape from my split self, for the White father has become a part of me, and I am in his shadow. But I am learning to no longer internalize his shadowy perspectives.

In unmasking my past, I undertake a process of re-presentation, restoring my perspectives in a way that is both indigenous to my culture and cognizant of multicultural dynamics. I recognize that I "can't go home again." But this process, which requires grasping the process of colonization, marginalization, and reconstruction of one's own personal history, means that I can now take "home" with me wherever I am. It transforms consciousness. In it are the seeds by which my split self is made whole.

How does a return to indigenous values facilitate multiculturality? How can it help Filipinos and Filipino Americans navigate in a pluralistic society?

Using Filipino language as a framework opens up a symbolic order where the historical determinism of colonialism is deconstructed. Though, on the one hand, the colonization of Filipinos seems total, there is a deeply rooted, primordial sense of self which can only be explained in Filipino language, not English language.

In the language of my colonizer, my culture is described as one based on "a collective sense of shame and face-saving." They describe it as marked by "reciprocity and the exchange of favors," and say it places "ultimate value on smooth interpersonal relationships."

In my own language, my cultural self-understanding is very different and much richer. It is oriented around *loob* (a sense of inferiority), *kapuwa* (the shared inner self), and *diwa* (psyche). Contrary to the construction of Western anthropologists, Filipino psychology and philosophies assert that the Filipino has a holistic worldview and perceives herself as holistic from an interior dimension operating under harmony (*loob*).

Colonization has overdetermined the Filipino from without. She is born a split subject, and she is born on the border of many intersecting cultures. Yet the indigenous consciousness expressed in *diwa*, *kapwa*, and *loob* is the predominant determinant of Filipino character, cultural values, and traditions.

In the United States, a growing sense of cultural nationalism among Filipino Americans resulting from access to indigenous psychology has been a way of suturing the split self. It has also been a defiant way to resist total assimilation. While remaining conscious of the limits to assimilation imposed by racism and applying learned strategies of navigating the dominant culture, such nationalism allows an indigenous identity to replace the obsequious, inferior identity which before had no access to its own strength and integrity.

The Filipino perceives herself or himself as someone who feels, wills, thinks, and acts as a whole. Out of this sense of self—which enables one to live on the border without becoming schizophrenic—is born the Filipino American's ability to maintain a sense of belonging both to a homeland and to an adopted culture. This ability is aided by breaking from historical determinations and psychological definitions imposed from the West.

We must nurture this reclaimed sense of ethnic self—or it will be obliterated. We must question emerging re-configurations of the global order, asking how these proposed reconfigurations will empower third-world peoples who are still fighting for rights in their own territories. We must always be suspicious of concepts formulated by Western anthropologists in the name of interdependence and interconnectedness.

We must also question whether it is really possible at this historical moment to have no grounding in a determining culture or history. In the Philippines (a post-colonial context), where the displacement of the colonizer's narratives is a fairly recent development, new narratives formulated by Filipinos for themselves must be allowed to sink and take root in the collective consciousness of the people, while keeping a vision of the global community. One must reach both backward and forward to maintain a sense of balance and harmony.

Mount Pinatubo slept for six hundred years. While it slept, it provided a home for the Aetas. On its slopes they planted, hunted, and lived undisturbed for centuries. In the lowlands, it provided a home for Clark Air Base and an entire city that supported this vast colonial-military enterprise.

Mount Pinatubo's eruption literally and metaphorically highlights the ambivalent struggle before us. Tribal people have been forced to the lowlands, and the U.S. troops have left. How will indigenous and imperial values conflict in this new, emerging cultural borderland? How will tribal people now cope with the forced assimilation into the culture of the lowlands? The town around the air force base is a tourist site for foreign men, raising anew the old colonial dilemma. Even if we want to recover from colonialism, will we able to? The master may have left, but behind the master is a long colonial legacy.

In the growing indigenization movement, I find hope. It reconstructs a strong sense of identity and ascribes that identity with its own integrity. This sense of self will allow us to take a rightful place in the global community. It has a voice. It speaks its own language. With it, we will undo the colonial gaze.

Confronting the White Noise:

Mission from the Experience of the Marginalized

by Eleazar S. Fernandez[1]

Like Leny Strobel, Eleazar Fernandez both analyzes U.S. mission history and explores its complex relationship to evolving Filipino and Filipino-American identities. Drawing on his experience as a pastor and theologian, he extends Strobel's cross-cultural critique into the realm of theology and the church.

This essay has given me an opportunity to consider the complexity of cross-cultural mission as it relates to my experience both as a child of colonial mission and as a participant in mission work in the U.S. in various capacities: as an international student, as a mission interpreter (through the Mission to the U.S.A. Program of the Presbyterian Church), and currently as a theology professor at United Theological Seminary in New Brighton, Minnesota. I will attempt to highlight some relevant moments in this journey and the themes that I have wrestled with over the last few years.

---

[1]Eleazar Fernandez is associate professor of constructive theology at United Theological Seminary in New Brighton, Minnesota.

A Child of Colonial Mission History

"A is for apple." Apples are not native to the Philippines or the tropics, but this is how I learned the English alphabet. It was only the beginning of a long educational tutelage under the colonial and neocolonial regime of the United States of America. Early in life I was trained to think and see things from the perspective of our colonial masters, which included the Christian missionaries. In my elementary education I was required to memorize the names of U.S. presidents and the various states that comprise the U.S. Abraham Lincoln was often idealized by my teachers as a figure to be emulated. Students were told that in America[2] even a poor boy has a chance to become president with enough hard work. The colonial education that I received at school was also reinforced at home. I remember, for example, my mother making white Christmas trees. We would boil white bar soap and paint the tree with the white, bubbly, waxy liquid, or actually paint the tree with white paint. Others would wrap the tree with white tissue paper.

The U.S. fed our stomachs as well as our minds. As a boy growing up in Leyte (a southern island), I remember the occasional relief food supplies donated by the United States. They perpetually reminded me of the affluence and benevolence of Uncle Sam. We would bring containers to our elementary school to get free powdered milk, cooking oil, corn meal, bulgur, oatmeal, and flour. The American imagery that surrounded me suggested an Edenic place before the Adamic fall. Everything "stateside" (meaning "Made in the U.S.A.") must be good; it could not be otherwise.

"I want to go to America," echoes a line from one of the songs that the Union Theological Seminary (Philippines) choir sang while practicing for a tour of the U.S. I did not sing that line because I was not a member of the choir while

---

[2]Properly, America embraces Canada, the U.S., and Latin America. For most Filipinos, however, America refers to the United States. It is in this context that I am using the name America.

in seminary, but I sang it silently deep in my colonized heart. After serving some years in the pastoral ministry on the island of Leyte, torrential societal currents pushed and pulled me toward the "land of the free and the home of the brave"— America!

I first studied for a year and then participated in two short-term mission programs. During those visits I learned a few things about America, but I still felt like a "missionary-tourist." As a mission intrepreter, I was well-fed, well-protected, and well-treated. It was not until years later, when my family and I settled in the Midwest, that I fully experienced the other side of America: its xenophobia and mistreatment of "the other." It took a beyond-tourist experience for me to comprehend America's complexity, its warts as well as its promise.

Missionaries Are Not Universal People: They Bear the Imprint of Location

All missionaries experience the difficulty of being an outsider, of being a stranger in a foreign land. In my conversations with mission partners from the One-Third World, this is the one aspect of our cross-cultural experience I have found that we have in common: the experience of otherness. But my experience of living in two worlds—worlds with asymmetrical power relations—has heightened my perception that the identity and location of a missionary critically impacts the kind of presence she or he brings to a particular mission context.

I first became aware of the role of location and its implication for mission when I was an international student in the U.S. A professor of mine, who was a former missionary, spoke of the presence of "foreign" missionaries as a reminder of the "other." Yes, they remind us of the other, I responded, but the "otherness" that they *experience* and *convey* are not the same. Euro-American mission partners in the Philippines do convey the presence of the other in the Two-Thirds World context, but they experience a *privileged otherness*. Their otherness is the standard for which most Filipinos strive. This means that the culture, the way of life, the way of thinking and acting of the privileged Euro-American other is not marginalized but the norm. Given this logic, the privileged Euro-American other can expect the Filipino other to adjust to his/her ways.

The experience of Two-Thirds World mission partners in Euro-American settings is very different. Our otherness—our way of life—is often viewed with condescension. When the privileged foreign other tries, for example, to learn our language and in so doing mispronounces the words, Filipinos react with a smile of understanding and appreciation. This is not the experience, however, of many Filipinos in America. They are often ridiculed by both Filipinos and Anglos when they mispronounce English words. They are teased about their "heavy accents." In some cities in California, where Filipinos are heavily concentrated, intensive "accent removal" English programs are now offered specifically to remove any trace of a Philippine accent. Thus, while foreignness/otherness is experienced by both One- and Two-Thirds World mission partners, it is experienced in significantly different ways.

Though mission partners undergird their missionary presence on the same gospel (God's salvific love as made manifest in Jesus of Nazareth), mission partners who come from a location of privilege convey a distinct message and experience a different response than mission partners who come from the location of marginalization. This tells us that the message is affected by the identity of the proclaimer. This tells us too that the "text does not speak for itself": we not only interpret it but our identity interprets it.

Let us take the case of a white middle-class preacher invited to speak to a poor black congregation, and a black preacher of a poor congregation speaking to a white affluent congregation. The words: "Be satisfied with what you have. Do not be greedy," take on different meanings in these two different settings. In the first case, the one who has more is rebuking the aspirations for equality that those who have less might develop. Whereas, in the second case, there is a rebuke given to those who continue to amass wealth at the expense of others. Unfortunately, since the powerful have more opportunities to proclaim their message to the power-less, the asymmetrical relation continues.[3]

Mission from the Location of Marginalization

The challenge that Tom had to deal with in the Philip-pines is a real and difficult one. I admire his struggle to break with his white privilege in order to be in solidarity with the people he works with, especially his hermeneutical vigilance against "imperialist nostalgia" and other neocolonialist temp-tations. But while points of convergence exist, what Tom is struggling with as a mission partner is quite different from what I have been struggling with as a mission partner who is at the same time a marginalized other.

My discourse on otherness/foreignness tells me that mission has to take different forms in different settings. This leads me to ask a few questions. How is mission perceived from the point of view of marginalization? What is the mis-sionary presence of someone who must face his or her racial marginalization every day in a racist society? What image would I project among those who see me as a "Two-Thirds World" person? What is the role and task of a mission part-ner who is viewed as a marginalized other? What message do I have to proclaim and witness, and what shape does the gospel have to take in such a situation?

Overcoming what Leny Strobel refers to as the "colonial gaze" (and what I will refer to as the "white gaze") is a con-stant challenge and a task that I have to deal with as a mis-sion partner. The white gaze has many expressions; it is a multi-headed hydra. It appears in whites' forgetfulness of

---

[3] Justo L. González and Catherine Gunsalus González, *Liberating Preach-ing: The Pulpit and the Oppressed* (Nashville, Tennessee: Abingdon Press, 1980), p. 94.

their own color and location, in the assumed universality of their perspectives, in the tyranny of white normality, in claims to neutrality, and in many more subtle expressions.

Peoples who are not "white" are referred to as "people of color." So are we really to assume that whites are colorless people? Those who uncritically assume the white gaze as normative are not compelled to know other ways of gazing. They do not need these other gazes in order to survive and thrive. In the game of domination and peripheralization, it is the periphery that adjusts to the center, never the center to the periphery. Because the periphery revolves around the center, in general, people at the center do not strive to learn from those in the periphery, nor do they let their commonly held views be jarred from the outside. Most often, if they seek to learn from the other, it is to make use of or to coopt the other.

Those on the periphery, however, cannot choose to ignore the powerful; they do not have the option of not knowing the powerful other; they have to know the ways of the powerful in order to play the game and survive. When some of those at the center have the privilege of a tourist-knowledge about other peoples, they often wrongly believe they profoundly know and understand "the other." To them I would say, "we know you better than you know us."

It is a tremendous challenge for those who think they are superior to hear a message through the agency of those who come from the periphery, from the Two-Thirds World. When a challenge is made, those who assume the dominant perspective may refuse to listen by labeling the message as only "a perspective." In one preaching engagement I stressed the importance of diverse cultural points of view. An executive-looking guy came to me after the sermon and said: "Thank you for your perspective; you really think differently than we do." This is a polite way of saying that he disagrees with me.

The "white gaze" must continue to be challenged, even if the process is slow. In this struggle the mission partner is not alone. There are cracks and spaces within the dominant cultural landscape, and there are groups both in the church and in the wider society with whom the mission partner may establish connections.

Reclaiming the Third World Within

Thanks to Worldwide Communion Sunday, there is at least one chance every year for the church to remember its global connections to brothers and sisters around the world. On this occasion a mission partner is often invited to participate in the communion service and to pray in his or her native language, or perhaps to preach. This is important in the life of the church, especially to its worldwide mission. Worldwide communion celebrations have become occasions to reflect on global realities, our interconnections, and the global mission of the church. The churches have made use of the occasion to deepen the social awareness of the congregation regarding broad global concerns.

Much work, however, needs to be done for people to realize the global connections and implications in every minute of our daily lives. From drinking coffee, to buying clothes, to filling our cars with gasoline, millions of people around the world have been involved. And this "involvement" is often exploitive. Millions are denied decent wages in order to ensure our comfort and convenience. This reality is also an essential element affecting how we participate in any worldwide *communion*. The annual Sunday celebration must become a daily commitment to make the world a better place for all.

Though Worldwide Communion Sunday points to cultures on the other side of the planet, it should not blind us to the various cultures within our neighborhood. Real global concern comes only when those who are often "absents" in our midst are made present. There is no authentic Worldwide Communion Sunday celebration unless we deal with "the other" worlds within our midst.

Mission partners from the Two-Thirds World must help enable affluent U.S. congregations to open their gaze beyond their immediate horizon—to both the faraway Two-Thirds World and the Third World within. They must participate in making those who have long been absents—absents in the sense that their plight and experience have been muted—present. Their missionary presence must help the congregations they visit to recover the absents.

In recent years many white middle-class preachers and congregations have become interested in Two-Thirds World theological voices and experience, and this must be encouraged. And it should be encouraged not only in relation to the global Two-Thirds World, but in relation to the marginalized groups within the church's local context. It is easy for the churches to remember those in the distant Two-Thirds World during Worldwide Communion Sunday. They invite a person from far away, a foreigner, to preach or say a prayer in his or her native language—a language that they probably do not understand. This is the Two-Thirds World that most churches are comfortable dealing with because it neutralizes guilt without requiring significant risk or commitment. It eases the congregation's conscience, so that they may not consider or confront the Third World within the heartland of America.

Why are people of color and the poor absent even in progressive white churches of the traditionally mainline denominations? Perhaps some are organizing and forming their own churches. But those on the margins are also absent because they know that their experience is not taken seriously at Sunday worship. Even in the churches where they attend, they are absent in the common discourse of the churches (e.g., preaching). "One goes to church to hear the gospel preached to one's own condition," says Justo González, "not to overhear it preached to others.[4]

---

[4] González and González, *Liberating Preaching*, p. 100.

Contextualization, Globalization, and "Gobblelization"

After returning from an exposure-immersion trip in Appalachia in the summer of 1996, I dropped by a Thai restaurant in Minneapolis for lunch. The place was crowded with white folks. I assumed they liked Thai food as much as I do. While eating I was drawn into a sober and meditative mood. I found myself wondering whether these people who like Thai food would also like Thai people living in their affluent suburban neighborhoods.

Food is a common and often easily accessible entry point to another culture. But we often don't get beyond the food to understand a culture in depth. There are now numerous international multicultural festivals in most states in the U.S. Ethnic foods, dances, and other cultural presentations draw people to the festivity. "Celebrate cultural diversity"—this is a slogan of the politically correct. But why is cultural diversity celebrated?

There is a common discourse about multiculturalism which clearly reveals its underlying ideology (as perceived by the dominant groups). The discourse centers on the notion of *enrichment*, even talks about *mutual enrichment*. But can there be mutual enrichment between a culturally subjugated group and a culturally dominant group? Whose interest is really served by this focus on enrichment? Charles R. Foster and Theodore Brelsford's study of cultural diversity in congregational life rightly points out that congregations value the cultural gifts of members, "but they are viewed as *enriching* rather than *transforming* congregational perspectives and values."[5] This enrichment usually results in the enrichment of the dominant group and the continuing colonization of the powerless others.

There is cause for celebration in people's increasing awareness of the plurality of our world. There is now space

---

[5]Charles R. Foster and Theodore Brelsford, *We Are the Church Together: Cultural Diversity in Congregational Life* (Valley Forge, Pennsylvania: Trinity Press International, 1996), p. 18.

for Black History Month, Native American History Month, Asian American Month, Women's History Month, and so forth. Seminary curriculum has also moved toward increasing globalization, with courses being offered on "Two-Thirds World" theologies, black theologies, gay and lesbian theologies, etc.

These advances, however, are also shadowed by ambiguities. The once subaltern voices are now given space in the curriculum, but the old paradigm predominates. Courses that incorporate new theological voices are still referred to as "perspectives" or "interest-driven" courses, while traditional courses remain the norm. If one includes Two-Thirds World theologians in a major course, such as constructive theology, as I do, the common perception is that the professor is teaching liberation theology, not constructive theology. What this says is that the real and normative constructive theology is white male theology.

The globalization of theological education is also a welcome advancement, but its rapid growth is both exciting and ominous: it is ominous when contextualization does not move on an equal pace with globalization. And it may be the case, as argued by Robert Schreiter, that contextualization has moved more slowly than expected.[6] When theological contextualization does not move at least on an equal pace with globalization, the result is the abstraction of a particular perspective from its local context and its universalization to that of other contexts. Since asymmetrical power relations exist between poor countries and wealthy countries, the latter have the means to impose their local perspective. Thus, we continue to perpetuate the unhealthy relation in the name of globalizing theological education.

The process of theological globalization must go hand in hand with a strong understanding and practice of contextualization. A truly global theological education is also

---

[6]Robert Schreiter, "Contextualization from a World Perspective," in *ATS Theological Education 1993*, vol. xxx, Supplement 1 (Autumn 1993), pp. 63-86.

truly contextual. To be globalized theologically is to be contextualized thoroughly. To globalize one's world does not simply mean being globally informed and committed, but to experience the decentering of one's worldview, the reconfiguring of power relations, and the pluralizing of one's world. If this does not happen, what we have is not globalization but "gobblelization."

Dreaming, Struggling, and Doing Mission Together

The missionary presence of a Two-Thirds World person in a powerful and affluent country like the U.S. is crucially important. My experience as an other—a marginalized other—has given shape to my missionary praxis. What seems like an odd identity has been chosen by God as a means to convey the good news.

As one who has experienced otherness, I have known what it means to live in multiple worlds: the world of the Philippines, the world of Asian-American life, and the wider world of North American life. This experience has taught me to extol the blue skies of the land of the free and the home of the brave as well as the blue skies of the Pearl of the Orient Seas, and to listen to the heartbeats in America as well as the heartbeats in other lands. It has taught me that we live in one world/many worlds. The privilege of living in different worlds has taught me that we can live differently and imagine and reconstruct a world in which difference is not treated with indifference.

A new sensibility—a new way of being, thinking, and dwelling—has sprouted from the desert of my experience of otherness. In my few years in the U.S. I have learned at least two things: white North Americans do not "all look alike," and there are Americans of all colors who know what it means both to love this country and to seek global justice. The solidarity of these people has sustained me throughout the years in my mission work. Our partnership, our work together to build a more just and peaceful world, is a response of gratitude to the love of God.

COMING
HOME

IV

There are cultures on this planet that have no word for minute or hour, cultures where a moment can last a whole morning. We don't live in one of them. In our culture the efficient and productive use of time has become high art. If you can balance three spinning plates on three thin sticks, you are rewarded with a fourth plate. And then a fifth.

Stephan Rechtschaffen[1]

Life is short. So move very slowly.

Thai saying

No Time or Space to Listen

L uisa Cariño, a Filipina poet teaching in Chicago, tells a story that occurred during her first few weeks in the U.S. She was waiting for the elevator on the fifth floor. When the elevator opened it was packed with people. Confident that a space would be made for her, that more room could still be easily created, her immediate reaction was to smile and squeeze in. But when she moved toward the elevator, the expressions and body language of those already on board suggested that there was no more room—that the elevator was *full*. She felt excluded.

---

[1]Stephan Rechtschaffen, "Why an Empty Hour Scares Us," *Utne Reader* 61 (Jan./Feb., 1994), pp. 64-65, excerpted from *Psychology Today* (Nov./Dec., 1993).

I could contrast her elevator experience with mine on *jeepneys* in her homeland. A primary form of public transportation in the Philippines, jeepneys were ingeniously developed from the U.S. military jeeps left during World War II. Filipinos extended and covered the back beds, so that from ten to twelve people can squeeze in on parallel benches. There also usually are three or four passengers riding in front with the driver, often including one on the driver's left (squeezed between the steering wheel and the door). A backboard is sometimes added to fit in two or three more, and three or four more people might ride on top of the load that is strapped onto the roof.

On visits to nearby villages we usually took jeepneys. When we located the right one, we would tentatively peek in the back to see ten or so patiently contorted bodies, a few well-behaved chickens, a sloshing pail of crabs, and several bamboo baskets brimming with tomatoes, okra, and garlic. As we moved to climb in, people immediately began to shift their bodies and move their possessions to create space for us. There was always enough room.

This was a much different sense of public space than Luisa had experienced on the elevator. On the jeepney, creating space was a given, even for outsiders such as ourselves. The high number of riders was partly due to the driver's financial needs, since the more riders, the more money he made. But it also was clear that most of the riders were willing to make space so no one would have to wait for the next jeep (which sometimes was a long wait).

Readjusting to individual space as a private commodity (and the primacy of individual autonomy) was different from but not unrelated to our return encounter with U.S. telecommunications. On the phone, as in the elevator, we discovered that Americans often strive to avoid human contact. When we returned to the U.S., we had to do a lot of basic things: reconnect with friends, decide on where we'd live, find an apartment, buy a car, take out a loan, Carol had to find a job, and more. All of this required making a lot of phone calls. We had only been gone from the U.S. for eighteen months, but when we left it hadn't seemed that everyone we knew had answering machines or that all businesses relied on tape-recorded voices offering numerical response menus. I thought I remembered that before we left, human beings occasionally would pick up the phone receiver and say "Hello" in real time. In the Philippines, it wasn't possible to "be" some place that you weren't, to be two or three places at the same time due to answering machines, voice mail, E-mail, fax machines and other hi-tech devices. Like most people in Laoag, we didn't have a telephone.[2]

"Reach out and touch someone..." in cyberspace. Though communication technology in the U.S. had proceeded at a frenetic pace while we were away, it seemed to be more about reaching out than touching. More than ten times as many people have call waiting and answering machines today than did a decade ago. Sales of cellular phones and Internet accounts (E-mail) are booming. I discovered that many of my friends and colleagues were now simultaneously many places most of the time—on voice mail in two or more locations, in cyberspace, and of course in some real, actual location.

Recently I saw an AT&T commercial on TV where a young businessman is rushing from the office to his son's soccer game while simultaneously listening to his daughter's piano recital via a cellular phone (his wife is at the recital with her cellular and is holding the phone up so he can hear). This image of the "successful" (affluent) American as a constantly

---

[2]Currently there are approximately 2.5 telephone lines per 100 people in the Philippines. President Ramos, with massive foreign aid (including $125 million from the World Bank) hopes to raise that level to ten lines per 100 people by 1998. Most of these new lines will be located in Metro Manila and serve the business community rather than the provinces. Eighty-two percent of the Philippines' municipalities are still without phone service. For a more complete review of Philippines tele-communcations see Gerald Sussman's article, "Transnational Communications and the Independent State," *Journal of Communications* 45 (4), (Autumn, 1995), pp. 89-105.

moving task juggler who is unable to *be* with his children and wife in the here and now troubled me. He is perhaps amazingly productive, but what is he producing, and why?

I assume a primary goal of evolving computer and communication technology is dramatically increased accessibility. Accessibility catalyzes greater productivity, which leads to bigger profits, the bottom line. "Money talks," and Americans have learned to listen with a myopic intensity. This is not to imply that people don't listen to money in the Philippines or other less technologically developed countries. They do—intently. They have to. Many struggle for daily survival. But they listen to other things as well. Perhaps part of the problem is that technology has accelerated the pace of our lives to such a degree in the U.S. that we now seem to uncritically equate speed and accessibility (the keys to heightened "productivity") with progress, and thus with a higher quality of life. But we have failed to connect progress with what we used to call meaning, with a comprehensive rationale, with an ethic. "Efficiency and productivity were [are] problems for slaves, not philosophers," Neil Postman writes.[3] They are also problems for all of us who are simply trying to find enough time in the day to listen to our families, friends, and others who need our unmeasured time and energy.

Though the Philippines is increasingly more hi-tech and computer dependent, maximum technological accessibility has not yet been elevated to a supreme cultural value, at least not in the provinces. There were no cell phones in the rice fields or at the market. I don't know if our friends in Laoag would have wanted them, or fax machines, or E-mail, or anything else.[4] They probably would, believing as we do that

---

[3]Neil Postman, *Technopoly: The Surrender of Culture to Technology* (New York: Random House, 1993), p. 25, (brackets added). This book is a provocative, insightful discussion of the effects on U.S. society of technology's rapid and frenetic growth.

[4]While we were in Laoag, a generous "sponsor" gave our college a new fax machine. But by the time we left (four months later), there had still not been a phone line installed and connected to the fax.

they will make our lives less complicated and more efficient, and create more leisure time. And given the long wait to get a telephone installed in the Philippines (a year or more), the cell phone is a simple (though expensive—$350–400 U.S.) way to avoid the tangled bureaucracy.

But it was the lack of this technological communication in Laoag that encouraged both deeper listening and the development of relationships and community. Conversations were not infograms or "productive" segments timed and scheduled on beeping computerized planners. I was reminded in Laoag that time is *not* money, and that money is not the most important thing that human beings can produce. Though communication (and life) was less technological there, it was not less productive. Administrators or teachers at the college would often send a student on a bicycle to our house with a note for us. Without other means, we usually walked or took a tricycle (a taxi motorcycle with sidecar for customers) to the house of the person with whom we needed to talk. In both cases the bearer of the message, a living breathing person, could convey not only the objective information, but the tone and intention of the sender. This method of communication inherently reinforced and nurtured relationships and thus community, as did the fact that Filipinos seemed to spend significant time talking with friends and family and colleagues during the course of their daily routine. This also fostered rich, productive lives—productive in the sense that human relationships and community were encouraged and sustained.

These contrasting understandings of communication and productivity are in part linked to differing understandings of time. People in Laoag were nearly always flexible enough to make space in the jeepney, but they also "made space" via their more flexible concept of time.

One dimension of this flexibility that I observed is what anthropologist Edward Hall has called a *polychronic* understanding of time. In *polychronic* cultures, many things, including commerce, can and often do happen simultaneously. The focus in these cultures is not on preplanned, set schedules, but on the maximum involvement of people and on completing multiple transactions.[5] This means that a community meeting or a worship service won't necessarily end at a prescribed time. It will end when those involved feel that their transaction, their collective experience, has been completed. The clock-measured length of the meeting is not a primary focus. Time is not a controlled commodity.

Hall defines Euro-American time, on the other hand, as *monochronic*. In monochronic cultures people prefer to segment and schedule clock-measured time. They select and sequence tasks and complete them one at a time. Promptness is important.[6] Time *is* a controlled commodity. Thus the quintessentially American solution to the problem of the increasingly frenzied pace of life in the U.S. is not to job-share, or lower our material standard of living, or live communally, or provide more and better day care, or underwrite universal health insurance, but to utilize "time management." We simply need to organize and incrementize our time more effectively.

Even though increased technology has westernized the concept of time in Laoag in recent years, I sometimes felt the tension between Hall's two categories: between my desire to have a schedule and complete a task in a given amount of time, and my hosts' capacity to juggle many tasks simultaneously—to spontaneously work late into the night to complete a task, or to shift abruptly to new projects. This relative flexibility was also apparent in terms of how events or meetings were initiated or ended. In the first few months (due to my own monochronic standards) I always felt as if I was either late or early. And though I eventually realized that

---

[5] Edward Hall, *Beyond Culture* (New York: Doubleday, 1981), p. 17. This "transaction" should not be confused with an ATM transaction or with a "task." Here a transaction is necessarily a *human* interaction, a conversation. The focus is not on completing as many transactions (i.e., "tasks") as possible, but on reaching a sense of resolution or closure that satisfies everyone involved.

[6] Ibid.

being "on time" was not the point, I still always worried a bit about when things would start or end (or *if* things had started or ended!).

On one occasion the juniors and seniors from the college were going on a picnic to a nearby beach. When we asked what time the bus would leave, we were told 9:00. Since we lived across the street from where the bus was parked, I watched for any signs of life. Some students and teachers arrived around 8:00 and began to socialize and drink coffee. Around 8:30 some got on the bus. Taking this as a sign, I hurried to get our stuff together and then climbed on the bus. Carol sat down on the curb to chat with Naty, a colleague and friend. They knew better. The talking and mingling droned on in the rising humidity. Between 8:30 and 10:00 students and teachers just kept pulling up in tricycles. By 10:30 there were approximately 30 people in the bus. The bus driver got in and started the engine. But before he could shift into gear, someone noticed that Jing, a junior class officer, was missing. One of her friends said that she had seen Jing the previous night, that she was coming, and that we should wait. So we did—for another hour. Finally, she pulled up in a tricycle, energetically apologizing as she climbed on board. Someone made a joke, everyone laughed, and we were off. No one seemed to mind. No one suggested we leave without her. The consensus was that it made perfect sense to wait for her. Jing was not "late,"and I was not particularly "patient."

In his study of the Ilongot, a tribal-language group from northern Luzon, anthropologist Renato Rosaldo also explored the implications of a non-Western or "traditional" concept of time. He reminds readers that "Indian time" is Western or "outside" judgment, which usually involves the outsider imposing his "clock time" on a new concept of time, which he therefore views as undisciplined, or flawed due to its indeterminacy. Rosaldo, encouraging readers to think not about the concept of time, but of *tempo*, offers a fresh perspective.

*In my view, optionality, variability, and unpredictability
produce positive qualities of social being rather than negative zones of analytically empty randomness....indeter-
minacy allows the emergence of a culturally valued quality of human relations where one can follow impulses,
change directions, and coordinate with other people. In
other words, social unpredictability has its distinctive
tempo, and it permits people to develop timing, coordina-
tion, and a knack for responding to contingencies.[7]*

Rosaldo also draws some important parallels to cross-
cultural misperceptions about time and productivity in the
U.S. He claims that those Americans who cannot conform to
our rigid standard of "time discipline" will be labeled as lazy
or unproductive because they live on what is often deroga-
torily called *C.P.T.* (Colored People's Time).

*"We" have "time discipline" and "they" have, well,
something else. The former quality of time can be described
in relation to cultural artifacts, such as clocks, calendars,
appointment books, and the like. More significantly, it can
be understood in connection with capitalists' desire to
discipline and synchronize the labor force, rationalizing
production and maximizing profits, but probably not
enhancing the quality of life.[8]*

In Chicago and in the suburb where I teach I often encounter racist stereotypes of people of color in the U.S. These
are most often directed toward Mexican Americans and African Americans but also include recent immigrants from the
Two-Thirds World to the U.S. The most common stereotype
is that these people are slow, unreliable, and lazy. This
misperception stems in part from a limited and ethnocentric
understanding of time and productivity.

---

[7]Renato Rosaldo, *Truth and Culture* (Boston: Beacon Press, 1993), p. 112.
[8]Ibid., p. 110.

Though time consciousness is increasingly more a question of class than race in the U.S. (i.e., it's hard to make money if you're not "wired" and digitalized), the stereotypes continue. A white taxi driver from Stickney, a nearby suburb, recently told me (first referring to Mexican Americans), "It's not really their fault. They just were never taught to work. It's a cultural thing. But the blacks get to me. They know how to work but don't want to. They just wait for their checks from Uncle Sam."

This kind of stereotype (ignorance) is tragically misguided—first, because most of the back-breaking, low-paying physical labor in this country is done by people of color, and second, because the Two-Thirds World is the first place U.S. (and multinational) corporations run to set up their operations to access a cheap, hardworking (slave-like) labor force. They relocate there so their corporations will be intensely more "productive" (i.e., cost-effective). Many U.S.-owned *maquiladoras* throughout Central America and Asia demonstrate this phenomenon. Workers cannot hope to live on their wages. In Indonesia, workers are paid 26 cents an hour to assemble Nike sneakers which sell for $70–$90 a pair.[9] A seamstress in San Salvador is paid 18 cents to sew a shirt which sells for $20 in a U.S. Gap store. In Haiti, the Disney corporation pays workers approximately 8 cents for each Pocahontas or Hunchback of Notre Dame T-shirt they sew.[10] The shirts sell for $11 at Wal-Marts in the U.S.[11]

Though "Made in the Philippines" is affixed to many products manufactured and assembled by U.S. corporations

---

[9]William Falk, "Dirty Little Secrets," *Newsday* (Long Island), June 16, 1996, A-4.

[10]Barry Bearak, "Stitching Together a Crusade," *Los Angeles Times* (Washington edition), July 25, 1996.

[11] Due to Robert Reich's anti-sweat shop campaign, and the tireless work of various labor solidarity organizations, some positive changes are occurring. The National Labor Committee is currently leading a campaign to improve working conditions in U.S.-owned factories in Haiti and Central America. For information, and to get involved in the struggle, write the National Labor Committee, 275 Seventh Ave., New York, NY, 10001.

in the Philippines, an even more serious debacle is the Philippines' *exported* labor. In an attempt to climb out of its poverty, the Philippines has become the world's leading exporter of human labor to the One-Third World. In Rome, Hong Kong, New York, Singapore, Sydney—in most of the One-Third World's major cities—Filipinas are cooking and cleaning for affluent children in order to support their own children at home. Many of these women have college degrees. Their spouses or sons may drive trucks or work as mechanics in Germany or Saudi Arabia.

The reality of this socioeconomic disparity between the One-Third and Two-Thirds Worlds, of the slave labor conditions and enormous corporate profits, makes the mentality of the Stickney taxi driver all the more frustrating. Though his point of view may be influenced by the inherent vulnerability of his job, his racist, intolerant perspective is not uncommon. As the U.S. rapidly becomes more racially and ethnically diverse, and as social safety nets are cut away, it may become more common. One wonders then if communication technology, and its inevitably wild escalation toward unimagined accessibility, speed, and information control capacity, will curb or catalyze racism and intolerance in our society. Will computers teach us how to listen? Will they foster compassion and patience? Will they help us to build national and international bridges between cultures? Can cyber communities replace the emotional voids created by broken families in the inner cities?[12] As technology continues to dramatically shape and reshape how we perceive reality, it seems we should carefully reexamine the relationship between reaching out and touching, between mechanical and human communication.

---

[12] Accessibility of a different sort is an issue here. Who will be able to afford access to computers and the internet in their schools and homes? As Jeremy Rifkin and others have argued, high technology is as likely to further divide the One-Third and Two-Thirds Worlds as bring them closer together. See Rifkin's *The End of Work: Technology, Jobs, and Your Future* (New York: Putnam, 1995), pp. 170-180.

Martin Luther King's warning, "Violence is the language of the unheard," is as relevant now as in his own lifetime. Marginalized and isolated from the wider society, young men across the country are constructing their own communities or "families" in gangs. They too are utilizing communications technology such as cellular phones and automatic weaponry (which are also increasingly *accessible*) to create well-paying jobs in the drug trade. Money talks, and they are gaining a voice in a society that continues to turn a dispassionate ear to their alienation and despair.

Euro-American intolerance and racism may be related to our limited concept of history, our growing lack of a collective memory, our failure to see the future in the context of the past. The ancient Hebrews had a view of time and history that might serve Euro-American society better as we evolve into a minority in the next century. They believed history was analogous to a person rowing a rowboat. With his back to the front of the boat, to the future, the rower is ever moving his boat forward, but he is perpetually watching his wake in an enormous sea, constantly considering where he has been. He is *facing* the past while moving into the future. Where he has been determines where he will go.

American innocence has been historically nurtured and protected by a conveniently selective memory.

Stuart Creighton Miller[1]

Beyond White Privilege

recently attended a Sun Dance on the Pine Ridge Indian reservation in South Dakota. When I mentioned this to an acquaintance, he became very interested and curious about my experience. He told me about his interest in Native American culture. He had seen *Dances with Wolves* and *Thunderheart*, was a fan of Tony Hillerman's novels, and loved Carlos Nakai's flute music. He asked a lot of questions. But when I described my experiences (not the dance itself, since that is forbidden), he seemed somewhat disappointed. They didn't align with his reading or other expectations: many of the dancers were recovering alcoholics, the sweat lodges were covered with plastic tarps and carpet remnants rather than

[1]Stuart Creighton Miller, *Benevolent Assimilation: The American Conquest of the Philippines, 1899-1903* (New Haven: Yale Univ. Press, 1982), p. 253.

118

buffalo hides, the sacred cottonwood tree was retrieved on a large flatbed truck rather than on horseback, the eagle feathers were purchased rather than gathered, the drummers used microphones and amplifiers, many of the dancers slept in nylon dome tents instead of tepees, and so on. My friend, like so many others, longed for the "traditional Indian," the "noble savage" that he had imagined and hoped still existed.

Renato Rosaldo would define this person's disappointment as "imperialist nostalgia." He believes that one way many "well-meaning" Euro-Americans escape or conceal their neo-colonial guilt over their historic complicity in the ongoing process of conquest is by "mourning the passing of what they themselves have transformed."[2] Though we belong to an extremely powerful, dominating culture, ironically, we often long for or idealize the cultures that our ancestors attempted to destroy.

Over the years I've noticed that there is a tendency for participants in short-term (one to two weeks) mission delegations to the Two-Thirds World to romanticize poverty. We may jet back from a week or two of "service" in Haiti or Nicaragua or Mexico talking about how much better the life is there: "they" are happier because "they" don't get hung up with "things," and because "they" live a slower paced life.[3]

Long-term missionaries, on the other hand, can't go home for a long while, so poverty is a bit harder to romanticize. One option is to simply try and avoid it. This suggests why imperialist nostalgia can be so alluring for returned missionaries (or others who have lived for extensive periods in a Two-Thirds World context). In retrospect, it was my capacity to *reduce* or *avoid* the hardships of daily life, to ignore

---

[2]Rosaldo, *Truth and Culture,* p. 69.
[3]The more obvious critique of these kinds of trips is their expense. Why send twenty people (novices), at $2000 each, for ten days to Central America to look around and try to "help"? Send the $40,000 instead. This reasoning contains two flaws: the money *wouldn't* otherwise be donated, and some returned delegates are changed persons, becoming political activists and advocates in *this* country.

opportunities to risk with our community in the Philippines, which makes imperialist nostalgia attractive now, after my return home. It can allow me to put a positive spin on uncomfortable memories and to ignore the reality of "white privilege."

The United Church of Christ in the Philippines (U.C.C.P.) has worked hard in the last decade to help foreign missionaries live with more cross-cultural integrity, to discourage white privilege. They are recognized internationally for having developed policies and training to orient and educate incoming missionaries so that they will not adopt culturally destructive or insensitive mission attitudes and practices. They required that we live on a similar salary to our Philippine counterparts, that our terms be no longer than two years, that we not assume leadership positions, that we study the local language, that we attempt to live like our Philippine colleagues in order to better understand the joy and hardship of daily life.

Though it sounds good on paper, this intended mutuality, this desire for co-mission, remained elusive. Carol and I did not truly cast our lot with the Philippine people. Our risks were relatively measured and limited. And I would be remiss in writing a book such as this without acknowledging my own susceptibilty to white privilege and imperialist nostalgia. And as a U.S. missionary teaching English in a former U.S. colony, I inevitably participated in the ongoing process of neo-colonization.

When a Filipina friend read an early draft of this book, she asked me why I avoided the topic of "white privilege." I told her it was much easier for me to recognize in the U.S., in the neighborhood where I now live, than in the Philippines. Initially, I didn't feel especially "privileged" in Laoag, though I did feel especially "white." Early on I was continually prejudged: as a cash register (a source of loans), as a G.I. ("Hi, Joe"), as unable to do physical (menial) labor ("We'll send someone over to clean out the water tank—it's a messy job"), and as an outsider/stranger (Was I the same tall white person the tricycle driver had seen a month earlier, or were there two of us?).

We were also continually misassociated with our predecessors, with the missionaries who had gone before us. Some had cars, cable TV, telephones, and obviously didn't follow U.C.C.P. guidelines. One aggressively collected indigenous Philippine artifacts to take back to a museum in his homeland (Germany). Students told me stories of his buying homemade toys from children in remote villages for his "collection." He told me himself he felt obligated to preserve their (Filipinos') history, because he didn't feel they were capable of doing so themselves. I presume this is the same reason he will park his exhibit in Germany rather than in the Philippines.

Though we were often prejudged or misperceived, we were also extremely and undeservedly privileged. Some of this privilege is the result of a lingering neo-colonial mentality (which seemed worse in the provinces than in Manila or other cities). Some Filipinos still mistakenly assume (due in part to the media and international marketing) that most Americans are one or more of the following: white, rich (this is relatively true), smart (highly educated), and physically attractive (stereotypically this implies blond and blue-eyed).

It was embarrassing at times. We were often asked to go first or sit in front at public events. On certain occasions it seemed that our hosts wanted us to be in a highly visible position, even though we had no role in the proceedings. When we could, we avoided this kind of privilege.

The real white privilege, however, was economic. Though we were paid a salary comparable to our Philippine counterparts, we received free housing and additional money in a bank account at home (which we were not to use while in the Philippines). This "readjustment fund" (for our return to the U.S.) was more than our Philippine salary. Occasionally, on weekends or college holidays, we traveled to different national cultural landmarks (such as the Banaue rice terraces), which many of our students and some of the faculty had never been able to afford to visit. After a bad fire in our house the mission board sent us some money to compensate for our losses. Very few Filipinos have housing insurance (none that we knew). But we didn't need the money that was sent us. Neighbors and friends from the college helped us salvage a few things from our charred bedroom, found us and our housemates a new place to live, brought us some clothing and food, and genuinely cared for us during a stressful week. Soon after the fire, we discovered the luxury of a VISA card. They didn't take VISA in Laoag, but they did in Manila. We used it to buy a fan and replace some of our clothes—more economic privilege.

Very few Filipinos have health insurance. We did, and didn't hesitate to go to a doctor when we needed to. We didn't have to wonder whether we could afford it or rethink our monthly budget. Most Filipinos would have to cut something out of their life (or diet) to compensate, and many would simply not go to the doctor. Several people I encountered could not afford a seven-day course of antibiotics, so they would buy one or two amoxicillin capsules at a time, only as they could afford them. Once while I was waiting for my wife, Carol, to get vaccinated against rabies (at the one hospital in Manila that had the vaccine), the attending nurse described a man who had come in an hour earlier. He had been bitten on the face by a dog that he feared was rabid. He couldn't afford the vaccine, so he simply walked away. I asked what would happen to him. "If the dog is rabid, with that kind of bite, there's a chance he'll die," she explained. "Many die from rabies in Manila every year. We need a cheaper remedy."

Since my return to the U.S., the concept of imperialist nostalgia as a strategy for denying white privilege has become more clear to me. Many "multiculturalists" romanticize and exoticize "traditional" cultures by focusing on "native" dances, arts, clothing, foods—on anything but the more difficult multicultural issues like racism and poverty. As a culture we "celebrate diversity," but we pay little attention to how that cultural diversity is related to class, to a growing socioeconomic disparity in the U.S. We may be more interested in Native American pottery and rugs than in ongoing treaty rights struggles and the endemic poverty and alcoholism that plague many reservations.

Some New Agers and other Indian "wannabees" long for the Native American way, for a spirituality that can sustain them in a fast-paced, hi-tech, despiritualized culture. But due to cross-cultural ignorance, many don't realize that that spirituality is located in the very land our ancestors stole from the Indians, that *place* matters in Native American culture. Though we readily separate the land from the spirit, they do not. Armed with this newfound knowledge, how will we respond? Will we use our money and power to lobby Congress to support legislation advocating the return of these sacred spiritual sites? Some may, but many will not. Some prefer to pay for cross-cultural vacations, for "reservation tours."[4] We sweat, drum, and dream for a week on the plains, then return to our "normal" life. The cross-cultural sharing is important and positive, but the integrity of the culture-crossing is tainted because we share so little risk and take our evolving political history so lightly.

The recent Atlanta Olympics is a similar paradox. The media hype and pageantry were obviously carefully orchestrated to highlight the cultural diversity of the U.S. But ironically, as some journalists commented, the actual coverage and commentary of the sporting events was exclusionary, decidedly U.S.-centered. Though it is important that we

---

[4]Interestingly, this fascination with Native American culture has also been growing in Europe, particularly in Germany. Nearly 60,000 Germans belong to clubs devoted to American Indian tribes and cultures. German tourist agencies such as Lakota Tipi and Travel in Munich organize tours to South Dakota reservations. Understandably, some Native Americans support this kind of tourism as a means of economic survival. Some tribes even send representatives to rent booths at international tourism fairs in Europe. The point, though, is how do Euro-Americans move beyond tourism and exoticism and toward solidarity? See Timothy Appel's "At One With Indians: Tribes of Foreigners Visit Reservations," *The Wall Street Journal* (Aug. 6, 1996), p. 1.

affirm diversity as a nation, that we find hope in the U.S. multiculture, are we to believe the media's delusionary imagery—that there is now racial harmony in the U.S., and in the South? The dozens of African-American churches torched in the same region during the year preceding the Olympics suggest another reality.

At the college where I teach in suburban Chicago, I recently had my literature students read and contrast two books: Nathan McCall's autobiography *Makes Me Wanna Holler* (1994), and Chinua Achebe's classic novel *Things Fall Apart* (1959). McCall, a young African American, is a former gang member who had shot people, participated in gang-rapes, committed numerous armed robberies, and finally ended up in prison. He powerfully describes the degradation of his own identity and belief system in White America, as well as his remarkable turnaround to become a respected journalist for the Washington Post. Achebe tells the tragic story of Okonkwo, a prominent Ibo warrior in Nigeria, who must confront the arrival of British missionaries and the simultaneous disintegration of his own culture during the colonial era. Aside from more conventional literary analysis, my idea was to consider the parallels between the two protagonists, their rage at white society (and Christianity), their colonial (Achebe's Okonkwo) and neo-colonial (McCall) struggles to maintain African and African-American identities.

In general, my students enjoyed Achebe's depiction of Ibo culture. Though they didn't "like" him, many sympathized with the defiant, supermacho Okonkwo in his resistance against the white missionaries and struggle to retain his tribal culture. But though they felt Okonkwo was justified in his rage, most felt McCall was not. Whereas they felt Okonkwo was a victim of white oppression, most felt McCall, as a "middle-class black," had failed the system rather than vice versa. After seeing McCall lecture at our college, they were frustrated because he refused to apologize or "take responsibility for his actions."[5] They called him a racist because he was still angry at white society.

One student said that, given what he had done, McCall was lucky to be out of prison, let alone to have such a prestigious job. How could he still be angry? She then went on to point out that racism was "not an issue" for most residents in DuPage County (where most of my students come from) due to the relatively high education and socioeconomic levels. At this point one of the two black students in the class described how he had recently been followed for several blocks by a suspicious policeman before arriving at his own driveway, where he was questioned. "I live here," he had said. Apparently the policeman had not considered that possibility. The student had not been speeding or broken any other laws. He was followed into his own driveway because he was black. I have since heard similar stories from other male African-American students. After the class was over, a young white woman, tears in her eyes, described how her boyfriend (an African American) had recently been harrassed and headbutted in the face by the leader of a skinhead group in front of a local public library in broad daylight.

As I tried to weave together these and other related experiences, I wondered about the students' responses to the two authors. Perhaps due to imperialist nostalgia (or a more general form of multicultural romanticism) it was less threatening to read Achebe, to get lost in the exotic tribal life of another era on a different continent. This was easier to take than the profound fear that McCall's honesty evokes in white America, and the depth of violence that his life represents. Students get enough "urban reality" every night on the six o'clock news reports. Listening to McCall's story was harder and riskier than listening to Achebe's because it was closer to home.

---

[5]Henry Louis Gates, Jr., responds in depth to these issues in "Bad Influence," *The New Yorker* (March 7, 1994), pp. 94-98, an extensive review of *Makes Me Wanna Holler.*

The frustrating thing was not that students disagreed with many of McCall's positions and attitudes. I also found his analysis limited, and I felt he missed many rare educative opportunities. But I was most disappointed by many of my students' quick decisions not to listen. They dismissed him. They didn't recognize the value of his story, or care how long and hard he had struggled to find a voice.

After returning from the Philippines, Carol and I gave numerous presentations about our experiences at churches and schools. We were sometimes misperceived as people who had sacrificed a great deal in order to "help" and teach poor people. Because most of the small midwestern parishes and high schools we visited had not spent much time in the Two-Thirds World or been educated about the evolving definitions of "mission" or "missionary," few imagined that we had in fact been more students than teachers, that we often needed more help than we could offer.

During this itineration period I observed that there was more interest in the Philippines as covered by *National Geographic* than in the historic (ongoing) political relationship between the U.S. and the Philippines. Mount Pinatubo's effects on the weather, Imelda Marcos' wild shopping tours, and tribal Philippine culture seemed to be the greatest areas of interest. A high school student asked if I "visited" Mount Pinatubo and when it would blow again. Someone else mentioned the Tasadays and asked if "they" still chewed betel nut and ate dog. At a small church in Arkansas, a veteran of World War II who had stayed in the Philippines for six months asked: "Do they still live in those little bamboo huts?"

Igorot culture seemed to fascinate many audiences. Their G-strings, rice Gods, and ritual use of chicken entrails generated more interest than the U.S. government's current push to regain military access to strategic Philippines ports via the proposed Acquisition and Cross-Servicing Agreement (which would give the recently expelled

U.S. military complete renewed access to the Philippines.)[6] Question: "Are there still headhunters over there?"

At the time there was a bill in Congress advocating offering U.S. citizenship to Philippine Amerasian children (most of whom are the offspring of U.S. military personnel and Philippine prostitutes who worked near the former U.S. bases). Question: "How hard is it to adopt Filipino children?"

We talked about what it means to the U.S. and Philippine economies that a growing number of our products are "made in the Philippines," and that the Philippines is seeking to solve its economic problems primarily by luring in foreign capital and investment. Question: "Have the Japanese started building cars in Manila?"

Maybe these kinds of responses are further evidence of imperialist nostalgia. Or perhaps they stem from the lack of U.S. media coverage of the Philippines. Or perhaps the Philippines is just too physically and psychologically removed to be relevant in Little Rock or Davenport. Or perhaps we all watch too many talk shows. I don't mention all of this to degrade any of the patient folks who watched our slides or talked with us about our experiences. They were exceedingly gracious people who, not surprisingly, had little knowledge of the Philippines (neither did we before we went there). Nor had they had much (if any) opportunity to consider the historic meaning of cross-cultural mission (neither had we before we became missionaries). But given the relative consistency of their responses, it became clear that on the local level mission is still widely perceived as "the white

---

[6]The Acquisition and Cross-Servicing Agreement (ACSA) would allow U.S. Naval ship visits and port calls, U.S. military training exercises, the storage of U.S. military equipment on Philippine territory, and regular replenishments, repair, resupply, and refueling of U.S. military vessels on their way to military missions. In short, ACSA would ensure a continued U.S. military presence in the Philippines (and Southeast Asia) in spite of the Philippine Senate's clear move (in a 1992 vote) to completely expel the U.S. military. For a concise history of ACSA and its current implications see Daniel Schirmer's "The Current Struggle for Philippine Sovereignty," *Monthly Review* (Oct., 1995), pp. 37-45.

man's burden," as an attempt to "do for" rather than "risk with," as "helping the poor," as a noble responsibility. These discussions also led me to the conclusion that many of us unknowingly engage to some degree in imperialist nostalgia and multicultural romanticism. Undoubtedly, my own selection of slides and anecdotes led in part to the audiences' interests and catalyzed some of their questions. To some degree, we all still cast "the colonial gaze" to which Leny Strobel alludes.

I have often wondered how we can ever get beyond this mentality. How can we ever learn to fully listen to another culture? How can affluent Euro-America cut through the white noise, relinquish white privilege, and re-imagine a more egalitarian society and world?

I was recently looking through some interviews I did in Appalachia several years ago. I came across one with Johnny Pittman, a retired miner in Claiborne County, Tennessee, with whom we had lunch one day. Having grown up as he did in Central Appalachia, most of what I've just written about "white privilege" would make no sense to him. He demonstrates the problem with labeling, with drawing conclusions based on racial generalizations but not carefully considering class. His "white" noise is completely different than mine. He reminds us that the only biologically discernible "race" is the human one—that whiteness, blackness, brownness, redness, yellowness, and other similar color designations are primarily social constructs used to classify and divide.

After Mr. Pittman and his wife had prepared an enormous meal of hamburgers, sweet corn, and watermelon for us, we sat on overturned ten-gallon plastic buckets on the front porch and talked. He shared some of his life philosophy.

"You come into this world naked, and buddy, you gotta leave the same way. We don't take nothin' into the world and we can't take nothin' with us. But you look 'round. Some people must think they gonna live a million years, all the stuff they got. I just want to leave my children some good mem'ries. The Lord supplies what you need, not what you want, what you need."[7]

Mr. Pittman, a 65-year-old white American with black lung disease, has much in common with many Filipinos. He comes from a culture of distribution and of profound hospitality. He is a deeply spiritual person. In his culture, relationships with family and friends often supersede material productivity. He has lived a lo-tech life of struggle and subsistence. Mr. Pittman comes from the Two-Thirds World in the U.S.

He suggests that the key to our learning how to listen, to our co-creating God's *kin*-dom, to assuring everyone a voice, is recognizing that we are all "naked," that we are all inherently vulnerable as human beings. This is what we have in common across cultures, and this is what we must come back to. Vulnerability is not weakness, and silence does not mean that no one has anything to say. But the world's resources *are* limited. How we live always impacts how others live. A culture of satiation will necessarily contribute to the creation of an impoverished culture.

These simple, profound insights come from the end of the holler in one of the poorest rural regions in the United States. Perhaps it is their simplicity and where they come from that makes them so hard to hear and to respond to. But it is Johnny Pittman and other missionaries like him who can teach us how to listen—if we will let them.

---

[7] Johnny Pittman, quoted in Tom Montgomery-Fate, *Bridging Worlds and Challenging Boundaries in Appalachia* (Johnson City, Tenn.: A. S. P., 1991), p. 29.

From Manila to Managua: Obstacles to Cross-Cultural Listening

After first emerging from the baggage claim area at Niñoy Aquino International Airport in Manila, we waded through the dense air into a sweaty mirage of gleaming brown faces peering through chain link fences. I was over-whelmingly reminded of the first time I had arrived in Managua, Nicaragua, nearly a decade earlier. The parallel would strike me again a year later when I handed my litera-ture class in Laoag the stack of 5 x 7 black and white photos of vendors and farmers from some unnamed country, and they somehow mistook Nicaragua and Nicaraguans for the Philippines and Filipinos.

During my time in the Philippines I was often reminded of such cultural parallels, of similar experiences I had had in different Two-Thirds World contexts, both outside and within the U.S. The following stories describe three such experiences. They all come from short-term cross-cultural "exposures": a human rights/solidarity (Witness for Peace) delegation to Guatemala and Nicaragua, a home repair work camp in Appalachia, and a seminary class visit to the Pine Ridge Indian Reservation in South Dakota. Collectively, these three stories suggest that listening to a new culture is always a risky education, which requires patience, humility, and the capacity to open one's self to the probability of being "wrong," to the paradox of strength through vulnerability. Separately, each story suggests a different concrete strategy for listening to a new culture, for crossing cultural boundaries with greater sensitivity.

Listening in Nicaragua: "Answers" Are Culture-Bound

Several years ago I co-led a Witness for Peace delegation to Guatemala and Nicaragua. Our purpose was to try to better understand the ongoing effects of U.S. foreign policy in the region, particularly as related to human rights issues. There were about twenty participants. We spent the second week living with *campesino* (peasant farmer) families in Paiwas, Nicaragua. Paiwas is about six hours from Managua in the dry season: two on blacktop, two on gravel, and two on dirt. It is also the end of the road. If you would want to go further into this remote mountainous region of Zelaya province, you would need a burro, horse, or canoe.

The third day in Paiwas we were to help with a community work project. Eneyda, the woman in charge of the project, told us to meet at the corner *tienda* (small store) at 7:00 a.m., and to bring a large pot or bag or pan from our homes, something to carry the sand in. So we did. Many were there early and all were carrying buckets or large pans. We waited and waited. We wanted to get going but weren't quite sure what we were supposed to do. Eneyda showed up at about 7:30 and didn't appear to be in any hurry. We were. Other people from the village started to trickle down out of the hills. By a quarter after eight there were twenty-five or thirty of us, and finally we could begin. Our task was simple—to bring sand from the riverbank up the dirt road to the top of a very steep hill where they were building a well. The three-quarter mile trek took about twenty minutes one way if you were carrying a respectable load of sand.

So each person went to the river with his or her own container, filled it, and then headed up the hill. This went on for about forty-five minutes (two trips) when several people in our group thought of an alternative and possibly more efficient plan: to have relay stations. There would be people posted every one hundred yards or so who would simply take the sand up to the next station. To compensate for the terrain and equalize the workload, the stations would be closer together on the steepest part of the hill and further apart where it was more level.

We tried to explain this idea to the Nicaraguans in our broken Spanish, how it would be a more efficient use of time and energy. They seemed to understand but were clearly not as impressed by the idea as we were. Some joined in and adopted our method, but at least half continued as before, making the entire trip on their own and keeping their own containers. We *gringos* stuck with our more "efficient" model. A few even speculated on how much sooner we would be done due to our innovative "solution." One commented on how much more "community minded" our approach was.

After several hours there was enough sand at the well site, and we went to the river to wash and cool off. Most of us thought the morning a great success: It was good to "work with the people."

That evening we discovered the depth of our misperceptions. Several of the Nicaraguans were upset because their containers were either missing or had ended up in someone else's home. This was particularly distressing to those who had only one large pan or pail in their entire house. It was essential to everyday life. They used it for washing dishes, clothes, and themselves, for gathering fruits and vegetables in the garden and at the market, and for many other things.

Some people were also upset that their pans and pails had been scratched and dented on the work project. Two of the plastic pans now had substantial cracks, and one had broken in two. This was due to our relay stations. With our plan, the container, which was heavy with sand, was dropped with relief on the gravel at each station for the next person. Under the original plan the bottoms of the containers *never* touched the ground. Each person carried it all the way up, dumped it, and then went for another. If you wanted to rest, you did it at the top or bottom of the hill, or midway, with the container resting on your head. This method both preserved the life of the container and assured the owner that it would not be lost or mistreated.

The moral of the story is that North American problems and solutions are not Central American problems and solutions. Some members of our group had found the answer, but no one had asked a question; they had found the solution, but no one had recognized a problem. The one-person, one-container method was the best way to move sand in Paiwas. It was the fastest, easiest, and most efficient.

Perhaps the other point is that the amount of real "help" a short-term visitor can offer (if any) in the host culture is directly related to one's capacity to listen and to follow, *not* to try to improve. Despite our good intentions, in this instance our group was more interested in sharing "answers" than in the real struggle of daily life.

Listening in Central Appalachia:
Sympathy Can Be Offensive

The Appalachia Service Project is an ecumenical work camp program for high school students and their teachers/leaders. Every year over six thousand volunteers come from all over the United States to do home repair for a week in Central Appalachia (in Virginia, West Virginia, Tennessee,

Kentucky, or North Carolina). Though there are many other religious and secular work camp programs for high school students across the country, few (if any) touch so many lives.

My wife, Carol, went on several of these week-long expeditions to Appalachia while in high school and then returned in graduate school to be on the summer staff as a site leader (overseeing and supervising the groups that came to a particular location). In 1991, with Carol's help, I explored the Project's cross-cultural education methodology. I spent several weeks interviewing both the volunteers and the local people (who owned or rented the homes that were being repaired).

Most of the volunteers I interviewed had participated in the project for several years. I asked them to choose one focused memory that they thought epitomized their experience in Appalachia, and then to write it up in a page or two. The following reflection, from Diane, a group leader, is one such example.

After standing in the Tennessee summer sun bewitched by the dazzling greens of the Smoky Mountains, it took my eyes a few moments to adjust to the enveloping darkness of the mountain shack. Tar paper, weathered cardboard, and an occasional plyboard formed the shell of what the eight-member family called home.

The stench of urine and chickens overwhelmed me as I stepped across the hard-packed, earthen floor into the home. My breakfast churned in my stomach, but I fought the nausea as best I could and pushed on. It didn't take me long to discover where the family slept. Two double beds lay crammed on the floor. Soiled blankets were awry on the stained mattresses. There were no pillows. A scruffy brown mongrel, hiding from the summer sun, glanced up at me from his spot on the bed. The bottom half of a third bed was visible through what remained of a cardboard wall. We had been warned that portions of walls would be missing, that those precious materials were needed more to provide warmth in the harsh winter than for privacy.

I soon became claustrophobic. I found myself gasping for breath, needing to escape. I stumbled through the dark corridor toward the rays of sunlight streaming through the shack's doorway. The bang and clang of pots and pans reverberated as I entered the kitchen. Mary, the hunched, toothless mother of the clan, was happily stacking the dented cookware, preparing for their move up the hill. The youngest of her four grandchildren sat among the clucking chickens in his dirty diapers eating Cheerios off the ground. I greeted the weathered woman with a smile, but inside my heart ached and my throat was tightening.

Could we do nothing for these people? Did a new porch, some insulation, the repaired stairs, and a downwind outhouse really improve their lives? Could we not provide something more? Some hope for the future?

The shock of the sunlight had momentarily blinded me. I slowly stepped outside, taking deep breaths of the clean mountain air.

"Beautiful, ain't they?" came the scratchy drawl from the aging woman I had left behind in the small, dirty kitchen. "I pity you kids having to live in the big city. Not having the mountains to wake up to. This is my home, my beautiful home." Mary sighed, reaching her wrinkled, fleshy arm out toward the mountains, urging me to view the surrounding hills through her eyes. Her gnarled, calloused fingers rested gently upon my youthful skin. "Pity."

Diane couldn't imagine that Mary might actually love her world and many things about her life just the way it was. This doesn't mean the old woman loved poverty or hunger or a leaky roof, but that Diane couldn't yet understand or fully appreciate Mary and her culture. The longer we listen, perhaps the more we will understand why Mary, the perceived object of pity, pitied Diane and the other affluent outsiders who had come to rescue her.

Many of us are like Diane. When we confront poverty we desperately want to "help," to alleviate the suffering. This is a good and admirable inclination. We are instructed by the Bible to feed the hungry, clothe the naked, and give refuge to the stranger. But in cross-cultural mission (or other kinds of cross-cultural work) this helping instinct sometimes evolves into a paternal, elitest, or even racist attitude. How does this happen?

Though every cross-cultural situation is different, the *motivation* for helping is worth considering. Why would people from the One-Third World want to "help" people from the Two-Thirds World? Though there are many others, here are six very basic motivations: (1) guilt; (2) a desire to control, manipulate, and gain power; (3) pity; (4) a desire to proselytize or "save" non-Christians; (5) a desire to "fix things"; (6) a humanitarian and/or faith-based desire for socioeconomic justice. All of these can overlap and may occur on personal or institutional levels. And all are part of the history of cross-cultural mission.

If it is *only* guilt over our relative wealth that prompts our desire to help, the focus may remain on us, and it may be more difficult to achieve mutual respect and enter into mutual risk. It is also unlikely that we will be able to sustain our commitment for an extended period of time. Helping in order to reinforce one's own institutional control, or to manipulate a political advantage, is of course the most destructive motivation, because the "help" will certainly harm the host culture. So might pity. A pity-full person (the helper) will have a harder time listening and is more likely to prejudge and objectify the host culture. A desire to proselytize is a faith-based form of motivation #2—a desire to control and manipulate. If we are intent on "converting," how will *we* be converted by all the new culture has to teach us about God, other faiths, and our *own* culture? A desire to fix things is a seemingly less ugly motivation, but it too often leads to destructive results. This is in part because the affluent outsider does not always understand that discerning whether something is "broken," or whether it requires fixing, is a necessarily culture-bound interpretation. And as the preceding anecdote from Nicaragua suggests, once an affluent outsider decides she/he wants to fix something and that she/he knows how, it can become very difficult to listen. If a desire for socioeconomic justice motivates our work, however, we are better enabled to understand "helping" as a necessarily two-way process. As we work to surrender economic and other privileges, as we attempt to risk with our counterparts in their daily lives, as we realize that *we* need help, we slowly move from charity toward solidarity.

We can't know Diane's motivation, but we know she took a risk. She went to Appalachia for a week. She learned something about another culture and even more about her own. Her experience is an example of what cross-cultural educator Claude Marie Barbour has called "mission in reverse."[1] This is an essential understanding of the cross-cultural mission process for those who wish to move toward the idea of co-mission. Mission in reverse simply means turning mission upside down, moving from sower to soil (see chapter 2). It is about *being with* rather than *doing for* in the host culture.[2] The traditional mission process is reversed. The people missionaries once believed they had come to "help" or "to teach" in fact help and teach them. In the above anecdote the supposed helpers, the haves, the subjects, are educated by the supposed have-nots, the assumed objects of that help. Like Mila, the tobacco vendor in Laoag, Mary reminds us that the best way to "help" is to slow down and listen more carefully to her and her culture.

During the weeks of interviewing in Appalachia, I talked with or received written responses from hundreds of volunteers regarding their experiences with the Project. In the end I was intrigued by their responses to one very broad, basic question: "How do you feel about your week in Appalachia?" There were many unique responses, but most were a version of one of the following: (1) "I feel fortunate and thankful for what I have. I learned to not take my life at home for granted." (2) "I feel good that I was able to help someone." (3) "I feel like I got back as much as I gave."

---

[1] For a clear explanation of mission in reverse, see the chapter Barbour co-authored in George Cairns and Susan Thistlethwaite, *Beyond Theological Tourism* (New York: Orbis Press, 1994), pp. 72-91.

[2] Ibid., p. 83.

Since I have already dealt somewhat with the first two responses, I will focus on the third. This interested me, because it seemed to suggest that the mission was "reversing" itself. So I pursued the question, encouraging those respondents to give a concrete example of what they "got" or learned from the Appalachian people and culture.

Here are some of their responses.

—*The names of five different kinds of wildflowers.*

—*A bunch of gospel songs.*

—*True hospitality; that people are more important than things.*

—*How to do a lot with a little.*

—*About patience in the face of immutable circumstances.*

—*That you can recycle almost anything.*

—*That a whole community can parent children. They seemed to discipline and love all of the children. We have become isolated and individualized, reserving our affections and reprimands solely for our own children.*

—*How to listen better, and not just with your ears. I found that the Appalachian people listened very carefully with their eyes.*

—*That happiness appears along the way, rather than at the end of a long grinding race.*

—*About a deeper kind of hope, the kind you need to survive.*

—*That I won't appreciate my family and nature and the things that really matter unless I figure out how to slow down.*

—*That we're all the same. We all love to see and talk with our friends and watch our children grow. And we're all afraid of the same things, of dying before we grow old and losing our way in the darkness.*

—*That we're all different. I can choose to come down here and work and live for a week. But then I go home. I have great opportunities, a lot of choices. The question is, now that I understand the disparity of choice, how do I respond?*

The last two responses suggest the immense diversity in how different people respond to a new culture. Though opposites, both statements are true to a degree. The Appalachians and the volunteers have many things in common, yet they are very different from each other. The first response is uplifting and hopeful, the second stark and haunting. One young volunteer sees hope and unity, the other a nagging socioeconomic disparity that must be addressed. The second response is more difficult because it presupposes that we must live in a burdensome question. It suggests that we must continue to act, to do the word/work of God in our own communities, no matter where we find ourselves. Pursuing that "mission" may be much harder than returning to Appalachia the following summer.

Listening in South Dakota: History Is Subjective

A seminary course I once co-taught, titled "Cross-Cultural Ministry," included an experiential component: a week-long stay on the Pine Ridge and Rosebud Indian Reservations in South Dakota, and a visit to the site of the Wounded Knee massacre.[3] During that week I learned something about listening to culture and the limits of recorded history.

The public bathrooms along I-90 in South Dakota are marked by large, cement-pole tepees. I assume this is to remind tourists that they are in "Indian Country." Perhaps a state planner somewhere thought they would trigger visions of John Wayne or Kevin Costner, temporarily soothing the spirits of tired, hungry kids in the back seat.

Unfortunately, this crassly misplaced symbol of Plains Indian life, this misassociation of tepees with toilets, is also a

---

[3] A number of U.S. cavalry veterans of the 1890 massacre at Wounded Knee also fought in the Philippine-American war a decade later. When the U.S. military was accused of widespread cruelty against the Filipinos, Wounded Knee was sometimes alluded to as justification, as an example of "successful" brutality. See Miller, pp. 219, 250. A soldier from a Kansas regiment told a reporter,"The country won't be pacified until the niggers are killed off like the Indians." (Filipinos were often referred to as "niggers" by U.S. soldiers during the Philippine-American War.) See Miller, *Benevolent Assimilation*, p. 179.

metaphor for the overwhelming historical ignorance (as in deliberate *ignoring*) of Native American culture and history. Given this inherent cultural ignorance, many have found hope in the resurgence of interest in Native American cultures (both by Native Americans and European Americans), which was initiated in part by the 1992 quincentenary of Columbus' conquest of America.

In my own reading during that time (1991–93), I noticed that many European-American writers, scholars, and activists viewed the quincentenary more as an opportunity to critique the *white conquest* than as a historical moment of *red kairos:* a vital time for the restoration, nurture, and even re-creation of Native American culture. Our tendency, as well-meaning progressives, was to focus on our guilt, to ask "What is it that we need to say during this year of 1992 about the European assault on the Americas?" What we should have been asking is, "What is it that we've never heard and still aren't hearing?" This is the question we can continue to ask. The most meaningful thing Euro-American Christians could have done then and can do now is to be intentionally silent, to seek out and create space for Native American voices.

I first realized the discomfort of this silence when our class arrived at Wounded Knee. In my mind's eye I kept seeing the black and white stills of Big Foot and his people's frozen, contorted bodies. I wanted to fill the silence with analysis, with lengthy sympathetic explanations. I wanted, through my words, to ease the pain of those few acres of grassy rolling hills on the Pine Ridge. But instead, we listened.

Other than a small sign which once read "Site of the Battle of Wounded Knee," there is nothing remarkable about that piece of prairie, nothing that would cause a passerby to stop and take notice. The sign itself, changed by the American Indian Movement in 1974 to read "Site of the Massacre at Wounded Knee," suggests the continued white reluctance to accept responsibility for the near-destruction of the Lakota people and culture. As does the fact that the Pine Ridge reservation remains one of the poorest socioeconomic regions in the U.S. Unemployment and alcoholism rage.

Francis White Lance, a member of the Oglala nation who accompanied us that day, didn't hear the silence that I did. He heard the moan of the cottonwood, the grieving sighs of the prairie grass, and the mourning wail of the wind. He told us we could hear it too, if we could learn to listen.

We tried. He explained how the battle occurred. He pointed out where the cavalry camped and how they attacked. How his ancestor, White Lance, and other Lakota warriors distracted the soldiers so some of the women and children could escape through the deep, jagged ravines that crisscrossed the valley beneath us.

He gave us a history lesson. He described documented testimonies which confirm that a Lakota-speaking U.S. cavalry officer, a friend of White Lance, warned him early on the morning of the massacre that violence was imminent, that the soldiers were all still drunk from the previous night, and that there was a reason they had brought the Hotchkiss guns. The officer encouraged White Lance and the rest of the Indians to flee while they still could, while the soldiers were still drunk.

For years historians have focused on and bickered over the initiation of the gunfire that prompted the massacre at Wounded Knee. Was it the cavalry or Yellow Bird and his men who catalyzed the shooting, which began while the soldiers were confiscating the Indians' guns?

Some say Yellow Bird signaled the other warriors to open fire with rifles supposedly hidden beneath their "ghost shirts." Others say Yellow Bird simply started ghost dancing, and the cavalry got jumpy and opened fire. Still others claim Black Coyote, a young, deaf, Minecongou who was unwilling to give up his Winchester, inadvertently fired the rifle as soldiers tried to wrestle it away from him, thus initiating the gunfire and subsequent Hotchkiss hailstorm.

But given White Lance's version of the story, passed on by Francis (and by other historians), it is worth considering the existing conditions and the cavalry's seemingly clear agenda.[4] The massacre may very well have been ordered days before. Perhaps this is why the soldiers all got drunk the night before—to temporarily forget about the brutal act they were about to commit. Why else would they bring the Hotchkiss guns? In *Wiping the Tears of Seven Generations*, a recent video about the massacre, this position was reinforced by a startling piece of previously unvoiced history.[5] In the documentary, Dwayne Blindman, the great-grandson of an eyewitness to the 1890 massacre, reads a portion of his great-grandfather's letter. It describes how the shooting began. The letter claims that a "black robe" (a white Catholic priest) actually read the Indians their last rites just before the Hotchkiss guns began to fire. But because the priest spoke in English, none of the Lakota understood that he was praying for their souls. Normally the army would have used an interpreter, but there was none used that day. According to the letter, after the prayer was read, a soldier yelled loudly twice and the Hotchkiss guns began to fire soon thereafter.

This insight has not made its way into any history texts. It is an example of a Native American voice not deemed worthy of Euro-American ink. Dwayne Blindman, Francis White Lance, and others like them, who are reviving oral traditions, remind us that it is the *listener* as much as the teller who causes the story to exist. As Christians of European descent, we are historically linked to the attempted eradication of Native American culture, and the silencing of Native American stories. So the question comes: Who are we listening to today?

As we approached the grave site at Wounded Knee, Erica, a German woman who came with us, could tell that I was emotional. She imagined I felt the same way she felt when she visited Auschwitz. But I was bothered by her analogy.

---

[4]Dee Brown's, *Bury My Heart at Wounded Knee* (New York: Simon and Schuster, 1981), pp. 413-419, contains an excellent account of events surrounding the massacre.

[5]*Wiping the Tears of Seven Generations* (San Francisco: Kifaru Productions, 1992).

Only three hundred Lakota were killed at Wounded Knee, not six million. But Erica explained that numbers alone are not the issue. It has to do with motives, with intent. Why would the cavalry intentionally slaughter innocent women and children with Hotchkiss guns? And she reminded me that this was only one frame of a larger picture. Millions of Native Americans have been killed since Columbus arrived. From Chile to Guatemala, from Arizona to South Dakota, the numbers are unfathomable.

It was then that I heard the flapping. I was looking at the red, green, and black tobacco ties, the colorful prayers tied to the chain link fence that frames the mass grave.

I was reading the long list of names on the stone tomb when, finally, I recognized the sound. I had heard it before— on the playground as a child, at high school football games, at the post office. It was a good sound, a comforting sound, *then*. I looked up to see a torn swath of white cloth flapping wildly in the wind.

That was the second time I had been to Wounded Knee that year. The white flag had always been there. But for some reason I had never noticed it, never heard it. It is a difficult thing for us, the beneficiaries of the conquest, to hear. We sometimes hear silence because we know the conquest continues behind technological and euphemistic veils. We hear silence because we fear surrender and associate it with vulnerability, with powerlessness.

The white flag reminds us that we live in a moment of *kairos* for European Americans as well. It is a time for us to learn to surrender to justice. A time for listening.

+ + +

These three stories offer some ideas for how to listen to new cultures. They remind us that gifts can sometimes benefit the giver more than the receiver, that "charity" often reinforces unjust power relationships, and that culture, like history, is constantly changing and always relative to the listener or interpreter. They illustrate the reality of the eth-nocentrism, the white noise, that still exists in our culture. But they also remind us that race, ethnicity, and socioeco-nomic class are complexly intertwined, that *white* voices and culture (in Appalachia in this case) can sometimes be drowned out by the white noise of the One-Third World in the U.S. Finally, they suggest that many European Ameri-cans, who are used to speaking and having their voices and stories recognized, may have a difficult time in the near fu-ture, as the racial and ethnic demographics of the U.S. con-tinue rapidly to change, as "we" become "they," a minority.

"We stand together, alone,"[6] writes Richard Rodriguez, in an attempt to describe the complexity of cultural identity in the U.S. The melting pot has cooled, or perhaps it never existed. As a nation we are only now beginning to under-stand a difficult truth, one that Filipinos have struggled with for centuries: a nation's cultural identity is sometimes best defined precisely by its cultural diversity. Rodriguez contin-ues, "It is because we lack a vision of ourselves entire—the city street is crowded and we are each preoccupied with find-ing our own way home—that we lack an appropriate hymn."[7]

This book is not searching for that hymn, but for the people who would hear it.

---

[6]Richard Rodriguez, "Does America Still Exist," *Across Cultures*, edi-tors Sheena Gillespie and Robert Singleton, 3rd ed. (Boston: Allyn and Bacon, 1996), p. 331.
[7] Ibid., p. 333.

Afterword: The Evolving History of Cross-Cultural Mission

This brief history and extended definition of mission/co-mission in the Philippines may be useful in understanding the essays that precede. I attached it at the end to avoid interrrupting the flow of the more personal narrative voice in the wider text, and because it is meant to complement and enrich the experiential definitions I have already developed. The concepts of mission and co-mission will be best understood, however, via the evolving cross-cultural listening experiences in readers' own lives.

Mission" and "missionary" are words that people easily dismiss due to stereotypical connotations. Many perceive missionaries as theologically myopic, conversion-minded European Americans who attempt to "save" poor, unchurched, and/or unchristian natives from hell and from their own cultures. U.S.–Philippine history suggests that this perception, though now dated, is based in fact. The sword and Protestant cross *were* united in the conquest of the Philippines at the turn of the century.

In 1899, after the Spanish-American War, when President McKinley was considering what to do with the Philippines, the Protestant church leadership strongly encouraged retaining the islands. "The churches will stand solidly against abandoning the islands," the Presbyterian *Interior* warned. "It is imperialism not for domination but for civilization...our

145

Mission Board can teach Congress how to deal with remote dependencies...." claimed Reverend Wallace Radcliffe. "Has it ever occurred to you that Jesus was the most imperial of the imperialists?" questioned the *Missionary Record*.[1]

Two years later, shortly after the initiation of the Philippine-American War, numerous mainline Protestant denominations sent in their own "troops" (missionaries), and then divided the country up geographically among themselves for evangelization purposes.[2]

In 1903, when confronted with the American public's growing opposition to the U.S. military's brutality in the Philippines (i.e., torture and the indiscriminate slaughter of noncombatants), F. F. Ellinwood, the director of all Presbyterian missions, tried to ease the American public's conscience. He described the American conquest of the Philippines as "a providential event of the widest reach and of the most momentous consequences and on the whole a great step toward the civilization and the evangelization of the world."[3]

Kenton Clymer, in his work on the history of mission in the Philippines, chronicles the evolution of mission from this turn-of-the-century ultra-colonial orientation through the first three decades of the twentieth century. He reminds us that today's difficulty in defining "mission" and "missionary" is not new. At a key national Protestant missions meeting in Detroit in 1927, there was significant discussion over whether the terms "mission" and "missionary" were still adequate and appropriate. Some suggested that "mission" be replaced by "Christian world fellowship" or simply "world fellowship." At that same meeting a number of noted missionaries suggested rethinking the purpose and motivation for mission.[4]

---

[1] Miller, *Benevolent Assimilation*, pp. 17-18.
[2] The Disciples of Christ were eventually allocated (and flourished in) a portion of the Ilocos region. This is in part why, as U.C.C./Disciples missionaries, we ended up in Laoag many years later.
[3] Ibid. p. 248.
[4] Clymer, *Protestant Missionaries in the Philippines*, p. 22.

Henry Hodgkins, a longtime missionary from China, sug-
gested five new missionary motives: world service, with-
out any hint of racial or cultural superiority or domination;
assistance in the search for freedom; a fuller life for all;
patience; and most important, 'friendship' with all people." [5]

Hodgkins' motives are important to keep in mind, lest we wrongly believe that most missionaries were/are nonlistening, insensitive "heathen converters." Some were/are (to varying degrees), and some weren't/aren't. But the fact that "mission" was being reanalyzed and redefined nearly sixty years ago suggests that mission as cross-cultural listening (co-mission) is not a new idea. And Hodgkins' fourth motive, *patience*, is essential to the listening method-ology. Without patience (an intensely culture-relative con-cept), we may continue to hear only white noise.

It seems that Hodgkins, and other missionaries like him, focused less on conversion and more on listening than their contemporaries, even during a time when that orientation was much less supported, during a time when no one was "celebrating diversity." Clymer also suggests that some mis-sionaries in the 1920's and 1930's (the "second generation" of American Protestant missionaries to the Philippines) be-gan to support and identify with the nationalist movement for independence, opening at least some denominations to the possibility of a less paternal and more culturally sensi-tive presence.[6]

Perhaps these early progressive missionaries also real-ized that they needed as much "help" as they could offer, that they were learning much about Philippine culture and their own culture from their Filipino counterparts. Perhaps they had also begun to understand mission as a two-way cross-cultural educational process.[7]

---

[5] Clymer, p. 22.
[6] Ibid., p. 115.
[7] The "two-way" aspect suggests a key idea that I have not developed. Many Filipinos, the "once colonized," must also *unlearn* unjust mission

Cross-cultural co-mission is *always* a cross-cultural education, but the broader term, cross-cultural education, is not necessarily cross-cultural co-mission. The difference is that a missionary's motive or orientation toward his/her work is somehow related to his/her religious beliefs and experience.

I assume here that the best cross-cultural education is not primarily intellectual, academic book learning, but experiential "whole person" learning, knowledge that comes from the inherent vulnerability of a short cross-cultural "dip," (an "exposure"), or via a "near drowning" in a longer cross-cultural "immersion." I also assume that the best cross-cultural education (like cross-cultural co-mission) usually requires from the learner significant compassion and the capacity to risk.

What's essential for both cross-cultural mission and cross-cultural education is the methodology. That is the depth of the *listening* and what that act implies about how the listener views and interprets the new culture. Therefore, the approach that I describe here is not limited to Christianity or to religious contexts; it could apply to anyone who is attempting to work and/or live in a different culture. This idea is reinforced by the word the United Church of Christ in the Philippines has selected to replace "missionary." They chose *co-worker* and use this term in all of their related literature. Because this word was developed by the Filipino church to define the role and relationship of "incoming outsiders," and because it is less limited, less awkward, and less historically loaded than *co-missionary*, it is perhaps the best word to describe the kind of cross-cultural relationship I am advocating.

Nevertheless, I retain the word *missionary* in this text to both accommodate and challenge readers. I use a word that we are familiar and comfortable with in an attempt to more

---

methodologies. An influential pastor in the United Church of Christ in the Philippines pointed this out to me. "We struggle with co-mission too," he said. "Some of us still encourage paternal, divisive mission relationships."

overtly critique its evolving historical meaning and relevance for the church and the wider society. This is because if we are to learn how to cross cultural and socioeconomic borders with integrity, we must attempt to simultaneously look backward to our shared histories and forward to the history we seek to co-create with God.

Glossary of Filipino Words[1]

adobo: meat dish served with rice (the meat is marinated in vinegar and soy sauce)

anito: the pantheon of gods in the kingdom of Bathala (God). Also, one's spirit ancestors.

aswang: see *tikaklang*.

bagoong: a thick fish brine used to season various foods.

bakya: wooden clogs. Practical footwear for warm and sunny days as well as for rain and flood weather.

bakya: crowd, the common masses

banal: sacred or holy.

banca: a small boat.

barangay: a division or neighborhood within a village or city, similar to "barrio."

barkada: a group of close friends.

bibingka: a sticky, sweet rice dish that is baked.

bolo: machete.

calesa: a horse-drawn carriage used as a taxi.

carabao: water buffalo, used to plow and work the rice fields, also butchered and eaten.

---

[1]The definitions of any Filipino words that appear in Leny Strobel's essay were written by her and were originally part of a glossary included at the end of her essay.

jeepney: jeep with elongated, covered bed, used for public transportation.

lahar: ashy mud deposits left by a volcanic eruption.

mami and *pancit*: kinds of Philippine noodles.

marunggay: a tree whose tiny leaves are picked and used as a seasoning.

merienda: a mid-morning or mid-afternoon snack.

mongo: a small, round legume (similar to lentils).

nipa: a house made of bamboo, often with a thatched (palm frond or grass) roof.

pan de sal: literally "bread of salt," small, round, bun-like breads.

pinakbet: a vegetable dish including eggplant and okra and seasoned with *bagoong*.

puraw: white, or a white person.

sampaguita: the Philippine national flower. Tiny, white, usually single-petalled flower strung into a necklace. It has a very delicate, sweet fragrance.

sari sari store: a small neighborhood "store" that is often one room of the merchant's home with a window opening on to the street.

tinikling: the famous Philippine bamboo pole dance.

tsismis: literally, to gossip. In an oral, highly contextualized culture, it symbolizes many levels of interacting, social bonding, or an indirect manner of communicating.

tikaklang and *aswang*: Philippine mythological monsters. The tikaklang is a tall, hairy, half horse/half human who inhabits the forest; the aswang is usually a female who can sever her upper body from her lower body, grows bat-like wings and fangs, and flies around at night stalking victims for blood and revenge.